God is

Miracles

Look upwards and trust. He will provide a way

Lexi's Miraculous Story

Marcia Madsen Hansen

To Lexi Hansen and all those who prayed for her.

CONTENTS

Acknowledgments i

Preface iii

Chapter One – The Miracle of the Spirit's Promptings 1

Chapter Two – The Miracle to Believe in Miracles 11

Chapter Three – The Miracle of Hope 22

Chapter Four – The Miracle of a Grateful Heart 29

Chapter Five – The Miracle of Christ's Healing Power of
Forgiveness 41

Chapter Six – The Miracle of the Priesthood 51

Chapter Seven – The Miracle to Know the Will of God 60

Chapter Eight – The Miracle of Mighty Prayer 71

Chapter Nine – The Miracle of Charity 82

Chapter Ten – The Miracle to Know the Heavens Are Not
Silent 97

Chapter Eleven – The Miracle of Standing Firmly in
Faith 107

Chapter Twelve – The Miracle of Looking Up 118

Chapter Thirteen – The Miracle That Comes Through
Fasting 128

Chapter Fourteen – The Miracle to Accept Our Trials 141

Chapter Fifteen – The Miracle That Christ Heals the
Broken Hearted 150

Chapter Sixteen – The Miracle to Press On With
Courage 161

Chapter Seventeen – The Miracle of Repentance 173

Chapter Eighteen – The Miracle of the Whisperings of the Spirit... 187

Chapter Nineteen – The Miracle of Being Patient.......... 196

Chapter Twenty – The Miracle of Being Filled With Light.. 202

Chapter Twenty-One – The Miracle of Facing Toward the Son.. 210

Chapter Twenty-Two – The Miracle of Walking With God 221

Chapter Twenty-Three – The Miracle of Arriving Home . 232

Chapter Twenty-Four – The Miracle of Following His Footsteps 246

Chapter Twenty-Five – The Miracle That God Knows Us By Name 253

Conclusion – The Miracle of Always Remembering 258

ACKNOWLEDGMENTS

My family and I want to thank each person who fasted and prayed on behalf of Lexi. We are grateful for the love you showed us and for your unwavering support and encouragement. It is impossible to fully express our gratitude for the gift you gave to us. You have influenced our lives by your goodness.

My greatest earthly support was given to me by my husband Doug and my nine children and their spouses: Shae, McKay and Makana, J.D. and McCall, Shelby and Brandon, Cassidy and Daniel, Kelsi, Tanner and Amanda, Lexi, and Parker. Their love and support mean everything to me. They are the best of the best. I am blessed to be called their mother.

In addition, I am grateful for my deceased parents who taught me about the Savior. I know that without their help this miracle would not have happened. They were with us every step of the way.

We are also indebted to the doctors and nurses who gave Lexi the best care possible and who did all they could to save her life.

Acknowledgements

Most of all, we know that we owe everything to the Lord for His constant watchful care over our family and for saving Lexi.

The time spent writing this book has been a source of joy and love for me as I have revisited all the blessings the Lord poured out upon our family. As Mary did, I have "kept all these things, and pondered them in [my] heart" (Luke 2:19). I wasn't sure if I should write about a subject that is so personal and sacred to me and my family, but I felt urged on by the Spirit to write so that others might know to a greater extent that God is *still* a God of miracles. I believe one reason this miracle occurred is because God wants us to call upon Him more often and with much more fervency than we are presently doing.

I am grateful for the editing done by my daughter-in-law Mandy and for the suggestions of my daughter Kelsi. The bulk of the editing was done by Sarah Monson who also provided valuable and insightful suggestions that helped to make Lexi come alive to the readers, for which my gratitude is boundless.

PREFACE

My husband, Doug, and I met while we were going to school at Brigham Young University (BYU). Our apartments were across the street from one another, and after a year of courtship, we were married. It was just a short ten months later when our first child, Shae, arrived. Our life would never be the same again— in a wonderful but exacting way.

Shae was born with many complications. She was deaf, somewhat intellectually disabled, and had cerebral palsy. We were told by our doctor, who was a member of our church that if we had more children that they would most likely have the same disabilities or greater ones. He suggested that before we had more children that both my husband and I should receive priesthood blessings.[1] We had full faith in the blessings given to us, which told us that our future children would not have any problems. We then went on to have eight more children, who were all born in good health. One could see that from the very beginning of our marriage we have been blessed by the power of God in our lives.

---

[1]Our church teaches that through the laying on of hands by a worthy man who has been ordained, he can act in God's name to bestow a blessing of healing to the afflicted if it is God's will.

I had always wanted to have a family of five children, while my husband was happy to have just two kids, I was able to talk my husband in to having more children when I reminded him of his heavy work schedule and that I would be

the one taking care of the children almost entirely. And I soon found that I enjoyed being a mother so much that I didn't want to stop after the fifth child.

Eighteen months after Shae was born, my oldest son, McKay, joined our family. He was studious, friendly, and more serious than his younger brother, JD, who was born 18 months later. JD was playful and loved to tease but was very loving. They became Shae's guardians. No one would hurt her when they were around.

Three sweet but lively girls, Shelby, Cassidy, and Kelsi - who could have passed as triplets - followed in the lineup. They were best friends. I would hear them giggling and talking for hours after I put them to bed.

Lexi was born with the last set of three children. She was bold, athletic, daring, and courageous probably due to the fact that she was sandwiched in between her older brother, Tanner, and her younger brother, Parker. They watched out for her, she tried to keep up with them, and vice versa.

More than anything else, all nine of my children love the Lord and strive to follow Jesus Christ in word and deed.

We were not wealthy, which made having a large family difficult if we wanted to take the kids to exotic places. Yet we found having fun didn't have to cost money. It wasn't unusual to see our entire clan going for bike rides or walks in the neighborhood.

On hot summer days, we trudged up trails enjoying the height and grandeur of the mountains and the wild flowers that lined the path and carpeted the hillside. Eating our packed lunch in the shadow of these majestic hills, while skipping rocks in the crystal stream soothed our souls. In autumn, the spectacular color display continued to draw us to the hills. The cool crisp air welcomed the kids as they scurried along the path in search of vividly colored leaves, tucking them inside their bags to keep their treasures safe.

Even in winter we found inexpensive ways to bond. As silent snowflakes fell, the kids would trudge through mounds of sparkling snow, pulling sleds to the top of the hill before sailing down, splattering snow on their faces. Even when very young, Lexi always insisted on pulling her sled up the slope to the peak herself, only to see it slide back down without her time after time. Hot cocoa and a glowing fire awaited our return. We found it didn't take money to love, make memories, or discover the enchanting mystique of nature.

During the year the kids made homemade presents to exchange with each other on Christmas Eve. There was always more excitement for the gift they had painstakingly made then the one the present they would get from Santa. And I found it fascinating that even when we finally saved up enough money to move into a larger home with more bedrooms, I would find the kids all sleeping in the same room the next morning. They were each other's best friends.

Lexi loved being the second youngest; she was never in need of a friend. She followed her siblings' example and was good, kind, and pleasant toward everyone.

In Lexi's senior high school yearbook, parents were given the opportunity to write a tribute for their son or daughter that would appear alongside their child's yearbook photo. These are the words I penned less than a year before Lexi's accident:

"Lex has a contagious smile, radiates joy,
and is unafraid. She is faithful, honorable,
confident, smart, motivated, and beautiful--
inside and out. She's a tennis ace pro, an
accomplished musician on the piano and violin.
You are amazing!"

If I could add a few more qualities to describe Lexi, I would also say she is one of the hardest-working people I know. In this way, she is a great example of what a member of the Church of Jesus Christ of Latter-day Saints should be. For instance, as members of the LDS faith, we are taught to be self-reliant, or in other words, do all that we can to provide for ourselves while relying on the Lord, instead of others.

We taught her that if she wanted to go college or serve an LDS mission she would have to pay for it herself. From a young age she started babysitting to earn money and then worked her way up mowing lawns and doing landscape jobs all before she was 16 years old. She put away almost all of the money she earned in the bank. After turning 16, she started working two to three jobs, even though she was on the tennis team, in orchestra, and taking AP classes.

Her reward for paying her own way through college, gave her a greater abundance of the Spirit and a work ethic that prepared her for her mission and for life. Through her efforts, she earned enough money to pay for her room, board, and tuition - and still had enough money left over to pay for her entire mission.

Lexi has also always had a desire to help and serve others. In high school, she thought a way to do this was to get involved in student government her senior year. Her brother told her stories of new friendships he had made and service projects he had helped with, and she wanted to have the same experiences.

Lexi was well liked, had lots of friends, and spent tedious hours on her campaign, designing posters and creating a skit, but sadly, after all her effort, she didn't win. I convinced her to not give up and to run for a class officer. But yet again, when the tallies came in, she came up short. Losing twice isn't easy for anyone, and she took it hard. She came home in tears and inconsolable.

Knowing that there was much more to life than an election, I said in effect, "Lex, God knows you. He knows what is best for you. This is a time you need to have faith in Him and His plan for you. Not just faith in Him - but faith that He is guiding your life. You did all you could, but for some reason you were not to win. It's easy to have faith when everything is going good, but is that really very strong faith if at the first sign of any affliction in your life you give up? Trust Him. He does have something great in store for you."

She stopped crying, and her face softened. Being popular had never meant a great deal to her, but she had told me often that she felt like this would have been a way that she could influence more people in a positive way. That's what saddened her - feeling she had failed to do more good. She believed me and threw her tears to the wind.

Preface

Sure enough, God did have a plan for her. Just two weeks later she was called to be the seminary president[2] for her entire school. Maybe it wasn't as glamorous a position, but she was elated. Her face seemed to dance with happiness. If she had been elected as a student body officer, she never would have been given this opportunity. She was selected by the seminary staff out of hundreds of students. I believe she was chosen because of her unwavering testimony of the Savior and His gospel.

Truly, Lexi is a spiritual giant with incredible faith - a rock. In junior high and high school she made it a goal to go to the temple[3] weekly. She is also unafraid to share her testimony and has always made it a point to share it with whomever she meets.

Another reason I think she was chosen to be seminary president was because of her sincere and pure love and kindness she showed toward everyone. For instance, it made no difference to Lexi if someone was popular or shy, she was his or her friend, and showed genuine love no matter what. Many felt the influence of her words and actions.

---

[2] Seminary is an elective, noncredit religious class that teaches about God and how to more like Him.

[3] A temple is literally a house of the Lord, a holy sanctuary in which sacred ceremonies and ordinances of the gospel are performed by and for the living and also in behalf of the dead. A place where the Lord may come.

Besides Lexi's great love for people, she has a wonderful joy for life that is an inspiration to others. Her million-dollar smile and contagious laugh conveys this ability as well as the beauty of her spirit. There is a special light that shines from her eyes that is visible to all those around her. It testifies of her deep love for the Savior Jesus Christ, so it makes perfect sense that Lexi's favorite scripture is found in Moroni 10:32:

> *"Yea, come unto Christ, and be perfected in him, and deny yourselves of all ungodliness; and if ye shall deny yourselves of all ungodliness, and love God with all your might, mind and strength, then is his grace sufficient for you, that by his grace ye may be perfect in Christ; and if by the grace of God ye are perfect in Christ, ye can in nowise deny the power of God."*

She is the epitome of goodness.

CHAPTER ONE

THE MIRACLE OF THE SPIRIT'S PROMPTINGS

"I have called thee by thy name; thou art mine. When thou passest through the waters, I will be with thee; and through the rivers, they shall not overflow thee: when thou walkest through the fire, thou shalt not be burned; neither shall the flame kindle upon thee. For I am the Lord thy God, the Holy One of Israel, thy Saviour: Since thou wast precious in my sight, thou hast been honourable, and I have loved thee Fear not: for I am with thee." - Isaiah 43:1-5

I had read and pondered this stirring scripture from Isaiah just a month prior to the accident. But now these tender and moving words became much more than a beautiful script on a page, but also a personal message to me from God. They seemed to leap off the page and into my heart. God was speaking directly to me. He had not forgotten me and would stay by my side as I passed through this profound challenge. I need not fear.

The night of February 26, 2014 is one I wish I could erase from my memory. I was home alone that evening and had just sat down to get a quick bite to eat when my husband, Doug, came rushing in the door.

"The hospital called," came his staggering announcement.

"The hospital? You startled me. I wasn't expecting you here," I said. His statement did not sink in.

"They called me when they couldn't get hold of you. We have to go to the hospital. *Now!* Lexi was hit by a car." There was a touch of fear in his voice.

His words jolted me from my thoughts, and I bounded from the table and away from my quiet surroundings. I grew suddenly anxious and there was pleading in my voice: "How bad is she? What type of injury did she sustain? Where is she? Did she break her leg?" My questions tumbled out one after the other.

He shook his head and sighed deeply, "I have no idea."

I ran to grab my shoes and my coat as I tried to make sense of what he was saying. He seemed alarmed and concerned, but I couldn't accept what might really have happened. I thought he might be overreacting, and I wanted reassurance that indeed her injuries weren't major and that she would be fine. In my mind, they just couldn't possibly be considered fatal. Serious accidents happen to other people, but they couldn't possibly happen to me or my family! I was to discover soon enough that I was in for a rude awakening.

I continued my round of relentless questions as we flew out the door and jumped in the car. He responded in the same way no matter how I made my inquires: "I don't know; it doesn't look good. We need to hurry," he repeated, trying to appease me. His demeanor told me it was much worse than what I had imagined. He continued, "The doctor just told me that we needed to get there as fast as we could."

> *"Hast thou not known? Hast thou not heard, that the everlasting God, the Lord, the Creator of the ends of the earth, fainteth not, neither is weary? there is no searching of his understanding. He giveth power to the faint; and to them that have no might he increaseth strength." -* Isaiah 40:28-29

It was dusk and the roads were congested from commuters leaving work, but that didn't deter my husband from speeding and weaving through the traffic to get to Lexi's side at Utah Valley Regional Medical Center, about 40 minutes from our home.

Lexi was in her second semester at BYU. She was fiercely independent and had been excited live in a dorm with roommates she had never met. She was passionate about learning and would only talk to me about her classes - never about boys (they were dumb). And although she was disciplined and tenacious in her thirst for the knowledge, she

3

also had a playful and daring spirit that thrived on the intense. It wasn't unusual to find her scaling a mountain, rock climbing, or bridge jumping. But because she was extremely unassuming and humble, others would never know that she had a "crazy - adventurous" side by being around her. Yet if someone would have asked her about a recent adventure, her eyes would have lit up.

As we drove to the hospital, I immediately picked up my phone and called the ER to learn the extent of her injuries, which I assumed would calm my angst. I felt if I could just talk to a doctor that he would alleviate my fears and the butterflies in my stomach would dissipate. I even imagined that they might allow me to talk with Lexi

I was not at all prepared for what the doctor said. He informed me that a car had hit Lexi while she had been long-boarding through a cross walk on her way to class at BYU and that she had suffered a very traumatic brain injury as a result of the collision.

I gasped and pleaded with him to tell me how serious her wounds were. The doctor, hearing the panic in my voice, became concerned for my safety. He wanted to know if I was driving the vehicle before he would continue to apprise me about the extent of her injuries. I managed to keep my voice steady so that he would continue on. I don't remember everything he said, but it was obvious from what he told me that she was in a coma and that her chances of making it were slim at best. It was serious and much worse than what my husband had gathered from his short conversation with him.

My pounding heart roared so loud I thought I might pass out. I couldn't fathom that this was happening to my beautiful Lexi--who was good and kind and sweet to everyone. *How could she be taken from me?* I could not go on living without her bright spirit in my life. It felt like an out of body experience, like it was happening to me, yet it wasn't. The searing pain, the grief, and the sorrow were all too real. It was unbearable.

I had just spoken to Lexi earlier in the day, and she was happy and full of life. She had been excited for me to watch a video of her longboarding down Provo Canyon. She had texted me several times during the day to ask me if I had been able to watch it. Her longboard had been her means of transportation,

 but she also loved to longboard in the canyon to feel the wind in her face. It made her feel liberated and helped her arrange her thoughts.

She was a free spirit who loved the outdoors, yet she had also always been steadfast and immovable in being

obedient to the commandments. I remember many times walking into her room to find her stretched out on the floor with pen in hand scrawling insights in her notebook that she had just gleaned from reading her scriptures. One particular day she had been so engrossed in her studies, she had not heard me enter until I greeted her. This was her sanctuary, and it gave me a glimmer of insight into her soul. She was barely 14 years old at the time. Glancing up, she seemed happy to see me and even more eager to talk to me.

"Mom, please don't think I'm bragging," she began. "I could only tell you this." She took a big breath and let it out as

> *"My soul thirsteth for God, for the living God; when shall I come and appear before God?" - Psalm 42:2*

if gaining enough courage to tell me her innermost thoughts. I had always wanted to know what deep musings were behind her face.

She continued hesitantly, "All my life I have felt different than other people. That I... that I have a special mission for this earth life."

Her eyes pierced mine, needing to know she could trust me with such a treasured confidence. "Ever since I was little, I knew I was here for a special reason. I feel like I see life in a totally different perspective than everyone else. I see what God wants for us. I am not bragging at all," she pleaded. "It's just a feeling I've always had."

I studied her face intently. There was such reverence in her voice I couldn't resist bending down to reach for her hand and kiss her forehead. Perceiving now that she was safe, her eyes softened and she continued to reveal the hidden secrets of her heart, "I have such a close relationship with God. I *know* Him!" Her voice filled with awe. A marvelous sense of peace engulfed our space and sent a shiver down my spine.

Feeling a surge of emotion, tears welled up in my eyes. I wasn't surprised at her words because I had always seen the light of heaven in her. She had a believing heart, but until now I didn't know that *she* knew. I dropped to a crouch and wedged myself beside her and the bed, lightly running my hand through her hair before putting my arms around her neck. The Spirit was a warm friend, teaching us through the silence as a cool stream of knowledge poured into our hearts.

As I thought of these sacred memories while driving to the hospital, tears returned afresh and trickled down my cheeks. But I couldn't help but continue to think about all the reasons I loved her.

> *"A merry heart doeth good like a medicine." - Proverbs 17:22*

My Lexi was so happy and full of life. It was rare to see her without a smile on her face. I thought back to the night when I was sitting in the audience as Lexi performed a song with a choir of girls her same age. She smiled the entire performance and lit up the room with her cheerful countenance. My eyes quickly scanned the group of girls singing with her, but not one of them was smiling. Maybe

they were told not to smile, but Lexi couldn't help herself. Smiling was part of who she was, a joyful, grateful, loving person that shone from the inside out.

It was incomprehensible to think this light could be snuffed out, especially at such a tender age, and, as a result, I didn't want to believe it. My greatest happiness in life had been my family, and I did not know how I could go on without her radiant spirit. I was in denial, but the horror of what might be started to sneak into my soul, knowing she was in such critical condition.

Just seconds after I hung up the phone with the doctor, my bishop[44] called. He had been at the church with my husband when the hospital called, and he wanted to see if we knew yet how serious the accident was.

Although I was still in control of my emotions when I answered his call, my voice trembled as I tried to hide my fears

---

[4] A bishop is the leader of a ward, or congregation, and serves for about five years. He is responsible for the spiritual and temporal needs of the roughly 350 people in his area and is not paid for his service.

and pain. I blurted out, "The doctors don't think that she will make it."

My voice started to crack in desperation as I tried to fight back the tears: "Please call, text, or email everyone in our church and neighborhood and have them start praying for Lexi immediately. Tell them to spread the word to their friends and family and have them pray for her as well."

After we finished our conversation, I likewise called my children who lived out of state, who had already received the news from their siblings. At the beginning of each phone call, we cried for several minutes, taking comfort in our mutual love and grief for our sweet Lexi before I could venture to say a word. Finally, while weeping and with barely an audible voice, I pleaded with them as I had our bishop to call everyone they knew--their extended families, friends, and neighbors--so as many as possible could call down the powers of heaven on Lexi's behalf.

Ordinarily I am a very private person and don't often ask for things from others. Yet, in this case, I knew instinctively that this was what needed to happen in order for Lexi to be healed. Because of that impression, multitudes were able to join with us in prayer and fasting for her.

In the days that followed, their faith along with ours was strengthened by the miracles that occurred. And from that moment on I did "not cease to pray in [my] heart" (3 Nephi

20:1) "for all [my] thoughts [were] directed unto the Lord" (Alma 37:36). This was the first of many promptings I received from the Spirit to help Lexi recover. I know that "the Comforter, which is the Holy Ghost…teaches [us to do] *all things*" (John 14:26).

CHAPTER TWO

THE MIRACLE TO BELIEVE IN MIRACLES

"The same came to Jesus by night and said unto him, Rabbi, we know that thou art a teacher come from God: for no man can do these miracles that thou doest except God be with him." - John 3:2

When we arrived at the emergency room, I leaped out of the car and sprinted inside. A member of the hospital staff was waiting for me and took me directly to Lexi. Within seconds I saw her still and almost lifeless body.

Her head had begun to swell so much that others would not have recognized her, but I knew this was my Lexi. Her entire face was covered in cuts, bruises, and blood. And her lips had swollen to be at least ten times their normal size. A bloodied breathing tube was in her mouth, and, likewise, there was blood in and around her hair. It seemed that cords and tubes were everywhere. My eyes searched for any movement in her body.

The hospital workers shuttled in and out of the room. As I stood next to her, the truth started to sink in my mind. I was in such pain, shock, and disbelief that I felt almost

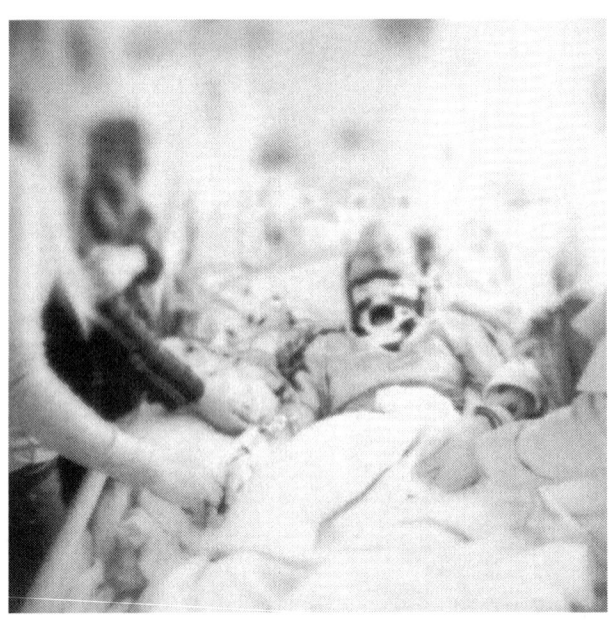

numb. I gently took her hand in mine, letting her know that I was there beside her and that it would be OK, but my mind was clouded with uncertainty, allowing fear to edge its way in. I felt helpless. I was her mom; I was supposed to be able to protect my daughter. Yet here I was seemingly incapable of doing anything. But a lingering belief told me otherwise - I wasn't powerless. I tried not to let go of that thought, but found it slithering away amidst the reality set before me. Grief poured in.

It seemed like yesterday I watched Lexi bound across the lawn, a cluster of dandelions clenched in her small fist. I could still feel the press of her tiny fingers against my cheeks as she laid a kiss on my lips and handed me the treasured bouquet she had painstakingly gathered.

The memory only intensified my pain and my fingers  tightened their grip around her hands, believing if I clenched firm enough, her spirit would not slip away. I was doing my best to hold back my tears, but they came nonetheless. Under the crushing weight of reality, my whole world began to crumble. My shoulders began to shake, and my throat constricted as the flood of tears erupted into sobbing.

Immediately, I felt the security of my son McKay's arms wrapped lovingly around me as he embraced me and held me tight. My family would be my anchors through this trying ordeal. My son Tanner, just two years older than Lexi, was the first to arrive at the hospital. He had a close bond with his sister and had watched out for her through her growing up years. Seeing her in this state had rocked his world, and he felt his heart breaking. The raw, grief-stricken pain I saw in his eyes, mingled with my own, deepened my sorrow.

Lexi's brother McKay arrived next with his wife, Makana. He had just returned to BYU to get his MBA at the same time Lexi was starting her first semester there. He had left home when she was only seven years old, so being in school together had given them an opportunity to get to know each other better. They both played tennis in high school, and now, after all this time and an age gap of twelve years, they became tennis partners for any match he could drum up.

My daughter Kelsi was the last to arrive. To her, Lexi's body

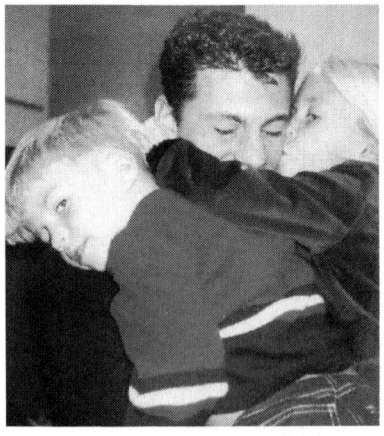

seemed strong, normal, and healthy - except for her face. At the time she remembered thinking, "Lexi is seriously hurt? Death was a possibility? That can't be true." She couldn't wrap her head around the idea that she was in a coma and wasn't able to wake up. She had

never been around death or even a serious injury, and now that it was staring her in the face, she couldn't understand it. Everything was very surreal to her.

She recalled several conversations she had with her friends describing Lexi. She would boast, "My sister Lexi is one of those perfect people. She is extremely pretty, talented, smart, righteous, and kind to everyone." And then she would always add, "She is like one of those people who dies early in life because they are just too good."

Remembering her own words, Kelsi felt racked with guilt, somehow believing this was all her fault.

After a few minutes, my husband, Doug, who had been

> *"If thou art called to pass through tribulation: ...if the heavens gather blackness, and all the elements combine to hedge up the way.. know thou my son, that all these things shall give thee experience, and shall be for thy good. The Son of Man hath descended below them all. Art thou greater than her?" - D&C 122:5, 7, 8.*

parking our car, finally joined us in the room. With our sons McKay and Tanner assisting him, he gave Lexi a priesthood blessing.[5] We were only given a few minutes to be with her before we were ushered into a private room where the doctors were to meet with us.

A heavy silence followed us as we exited the room. Stares of sympathy and sadness showed in the eyes of all who met our gaze, sensing our grief. I wanted to find a place of safety and refuge, but the dark clouds of uncertainty grew ominous. Until the door shut behind us, I had not noticed how much noise there had been until the commotion was gone. Everywhere I looked seemed bleak and sorrowful.

In a few minutes the doctors came in, their faces grim, and began to explain to us the grave news that Lexi had less

---

[5]In our church when a young man turns 18 years old, he becomes an Elder and receives the Melchizedek Priesthood. This priesthood gives him the power to act in Christ's name, to know the mind and will of God, and to have the heavens opened to him for the one who is afflicted. Through the priesthood, miracles can and do occur as men do and say what God would say if He were here on earth. The man places his hands on the head of the person in need and pronounces a blessing.

than a 1% chance to live. I sat motionless, staring straight ahead, my eyes burning as tears continued to roll down my cheeks. At the time I wasn't really listening, as my mind was racing and my heart was in turmoil. Everything was a blur like it wasn't really happening and yet it was. I kept on thinking about how this horrible accident could not have happened to my beautiful, kind Lexi. I could not lose her - not now, not ever. In my mind it would all turn out... it just had to! My heart was troubled; it was afraid (John 14:27).

It was the words my son said that finally startled me out of the fog I was in. I heard his words loud and clear even though it was spoken in a soft tone. He asked the doctors if we needed to call his brother and sisters home that were living out of state. The neurologist was emphatic and told him that we most definitely needed to call them home to Utah and asked when the very soonest the family would be able to get there in order to keep Lexi alive.

I was in shock! I had not let my mind even consider the possibility that she might not be with us anymore. I let out a grief stricken cry and pleaded, "Why? Why do we need to call?"

His statement had sent a fresh wave of unbelievable hurt through my heart. I knew exactly what they meant by their statement, but the news was too much for my heart to bear. I had realized Lexi had some serious wounds but nothing, I thought, that couldn't heal with time. The thought had only momentarily crossed my mind that she was in such critical condition that she might not live through the night. Like Rahab, "as soon as [I] had heard these things, [my heart] did melt, neither did there remain any more courage [in me]" (Joshua 2:11). I was starting to succumb to shock as I begged the doctors, "I don't want to be here. I want to be back with my Lexi. Take me back; please take me back to my Lexi."

After hearing my heartfelt pleadings to see my daughter again, a hospital social worker named Travis jumped up from his seat and said he'd take me back to her. His eyes filled with compassion. He accompanied me back to her room in the ER and stood with me by her hospital bed. Upon viewing Lexi's lifeless body, the tears spilled out, and I started sobbing uncontrollably, my chest heaving and gasping for air.

In an effort to help me regain control, Travis began to engage me in conversation. "Were you close?" he asked, cocking his head in sympathy.

I was hurting too much to care to respond, but somehow, between grasps for air, I began to haltingly speak. "She was my best friend," I said. (I am blessed to feel that way about each of my children.) "I can't lose her." There was a desperate pleading in my voice for him to tell me it would be alright - that it wasn't as bad as it seemed.

Travis continued in his attempt to calm me. "It's OK if you had harsh words before this," he said, thinking that was the cause of some of my pain.

I was shocked by the suggestion: "No, no. We were so close! I have no regrets." My voice seemed to beg for him to understand that she was different. She was near perfection and a light as bright as hers could not be replaced.

"I just can't go on without her. She means everything to me," I stammered, as the tears continued to flow.

An empty hollowness burrowed its way inside of me. I needed the ray of sunshine she brought into my life. Her cheerful voice, bright smile and countenance - they were what made my life complete. I wanted Travis to know that this wasn't just a body lying there with no name. This was Lexi, my daughter. She was my joy, my life. My heart felt ripped out of my body.

"What was she like growing up?" he questioned.

I could barely speak now. "She...She... was good... to everyone," I whispered, my voice stifled by my tears. The enormity of all that had happened settled on me with

> *"God is eagerly awaiting for the chance to answer your prayers and fulfill your dreams just as he always has. But he can't if you do not pray and he can't if you do not dream. In short, he can't if you do not believe." - Jeffrey R. Holland, "This, the Greatest of All Dispensations," CES Fireside, September 2004.*

massive force, filling my body with absolute and complete turmoil. It was the deepest anguish I had ever felt.

Travis, seeing how distraught I was, told me to take some deep breaths before I passed out. He continued to try to calm me down, but I was inconsolable.

Finally, he turned and stood in front of me, just inches away from my face, looked me directly in my eyes, and said firmly and with great intensity, "Listen, I have worked in this hospital a long time, and I have seen lots of miracles. You need to pray for a miracle. Above all you need to know that a miracle can happen. Particularly, you need to be there for your family. They are looking to you for strength."

His words penetrated my heart. Yes, that *is* what I knew to be true! The scriptures had always been a powerful influence in my life. I had studied them daily and knew the words and the miracles I had read were true.

God is a God of miracles, and He hears and answers prayers! Yet in that small moment, I had let myself go to a place of fear and hopelessness. In seeing my daughter's lifeless body and hearing the doctors say that she wouldn't make it

> *"And there were great and marvelous works wrought by the disciples of Jesus, insomuch that they did heal the sick, and raise the dead, and cause the lame to walk, and the blind to receive their sight, and the deaf to hear; and all manner of miracles did they work among the children of men; and in nothing did they work miracles save it were in the name of Jesus" - 3 Nephi 1:5*

through the night, I'd forgotten that God knew me and that He knew Lexi. She was in His hands. He *could* heal her!

Fighting back the tears, I was able to snap out of that state of despair and abandonment almost instantly and replace it with an assurance, a hope and a belief that God could heal my daughter and make her whole. I began to "look unto [God . . . to] doubt not, fear not" (D&C 6:36). And I realized I wanted to be that rock my family could lean on.

What I was experienced wasn't just a glimmer of hope but absolute knowledge borne of hope. Although still in anguish of soul and weighed down with what seemed the most crushing blow that I could have ever imagined happening to a mother, I had hope. I recognized that God could heal my daughter from almost certain death through humble and earnest prayer if it was His will that she remain with us.

I didn't get an immediate answer to such an extraordinary plea, but it would come, that I knew. God had always been and would continue to be my anchor. I would give all my energies now to calling down the powers of Heaven on Lexi's behalf for a miracle if that was His will. Through the depths of my despair, God had filled me with inner strength.

As I hesitantly walked back to my family, I fought to stay calm. And I began to muster the faith I needed for the Lord to heal my daughter, while still aching inside.

Travis looked at me and said "I can see a change in you already."

I had humbled myself to hear his counsel. My heart was opened, and I was able to invite the Holy Ghost back into my soul to replace my fear. I resolved to have the courage and strength I knew that my family deserved. My "eyes [could now] see afar off" (Moses 6:27). I brushed away the final tear that night with the back of my hand, telling myself to breathe slowly. I knew I must "cleave unto the Lord, as [I had] done unto this day" (Joshua 23:8).

Looking back, I have pondered about that moment. I know I would have eventually come to that place of faith; however, with Travis' help, I was able to get there immediately--and for that I will be ever grateful. God is a God of miracles and I needed to keep that forefront in my mind and heart from this moment forward.

CHAPTER THREE

THE MIRACLE OF HOPE

"Blessed is the man that trusteth in the Lord, and whose hope the Lord is." - Jeremiah 17:7

Because I had left the room to see Lexi, I had missed the doctors' explanation to the rest of the family about the magnitude of her injuries. So, my family gave me the details later that night.

She had contusions to her lungs, which are "bruises that can possibly lead to inadequate oxygen levels, resulting in [the need for] supplemental oxygen. A contusion plays a key role in determining whether an individual will die or suffer serious ill effects as the result of trauma" (Wikipedia). She also had a C2 fracture[6] on her spinal cord. A physical therapist at the hospital later showed us a skeleton to help us understand the severity of her injury. He told us that a C1 fracture would result in automatic death, a C2 fracture - if

---

[6] A C2 fracture is a fracture on the second vertebra of the spine. The C-spine is the most feared of all spinal injuries, and the higher the position of the C-spine injury, the higher the morbidity and mortality (Medscape).

broken completely - would mean the patient would only be able to blink their eyes. Luckily, he said, Lexi's fracture had not broken completely, so she could have complete healing if everything went well.

However, the neurologist stated that even all this was considered minor compared to the injuries to her brain. He explained that Lexi had experienced a shearing injury in the subarachnoid area[7] of her brain, as well as bleeding in either the epidural[8] or subdural[9] area. A shearing injury is when the neurons that carry electrical signals in your brain get sheared, or cut off from each other. These are vital connections in our brain that cannot be repaired once lost. And the bleeding in her brain meant that they would not be able to operate as the injury was too deep and the damage had already been done.

Later that night the physician's assistant pointed out little white specks on the CT scan and stated that these were the areas of shearing. One of us asked what percent chance she had of coming out of this.

---

[7] The subarachnoid space is a small space on the surface of the hemispheres of the brain and is filled with spongy, connective tissue and "intercommunicating channels in which the cerebrospinal fluid is contained" (Wikipedia).

[8] The epidural space is the outermost part of the spinal canal. "In humans, the epidural space contains lumphatics, spinal nerve roots, loose connective tissue, fatty tissue, small arteries, and a network of internal vertebral venous plexus" (Wikipedia).

[9] The subdural space is a potential space that can be created by an injury (Wikipedia).

He sighed and said, "Lexi has less than a one percent chance of living, maybe two." He went on to explain that with brain injuries they can never truly know the severity of the outcome. If Lexi were to make it, she may never walk or speak again. He said that many people who suffer brain injuries end up in a care center, never to function independently for the rest of their lives.

The neurologist then said that Lexi had been displaying "decorticate" and "decerebrate" posturing, and had even been transitioning back and forth between the two. Decorticate posturing is "when the patient's back arches backwards and flexes the arms, whereas decerebrate posturing is where the patient arches the back (like in decorticate posturing) but then extends the arms out parallel to the body.....Both decorticate posturing and decerebrate posturing are indicative of serious head injuries with significant damage to the brain" (EMP). This was grave news, and I knew we had "deep water [yet]...to swim in" (D&C 127:2).

I had only been back in the room with my family for a few minutes when my youngest son, Parker, opened the door and walked in with a heavy heart. He had not been at home when we had rushed to the hospital, so our next-door neighbor, was kind enough to bring him.

Parker had been so distraught upon learning that his sister had been hit by a car that he did not know if he could handle seeing her in that condition.

Sensing Parker's despair, our neighbor pulled over on the side of the road to say a prayer. He assumed that he would pray for peace and comfort for Parker and our

> "Be of good cheer. The Man of Galilee, the Creator, the Son of the Living God will not forget nor forsake those whose hearts are drawn to Him. I testify that the Man who suffered for mankind, who committed His life to healing the sick comforting the disconsolate, is mindful of your sufferings, doubts and heartaches." - Joseph B. Wirthlin, "Finding a Safe Harbor," Ensign, May 2000.

family, considering that from all accounts Lexi was not going to live. Instead, he felt impressed to ask our Heavenly Father that she would be made whole. That prayer was one of many offered for Lexi in which the Holy Ghost prompted the individual to pray for a miracle.

I was the first person Parker caught sight of when he entered the room, and he immediately burst into tears. He had been trying to be strong up until that point but could no longer hold back his tears. His first thought was for me rather than for himself as he tried to comfort me.

Choking from emotion he said, "'Mom it's going to be ok. This earth life is minuscule when we think about eternity. It will be just a blink of an eye, and then we will be together

25

again. That is what my seminary teacher told me," he said looking at me with kind and tender eyes. He sorely ached to have his sister with him yet, despite his own sorrow he was able to turn outward to comfort me. I was grateful that I had not let my heart give way to grief, so that I could be strong for Parker instead of weeping in his arms, when his soul was filled with such anguish.

I was able to give him a big hug and whisper, "No, Parker, don't talk that way. We need to have faith. Lexi will be fine. She is not leaving us. We cannot lose hope." Now with clearer

> *"Yea, and it came to pass that the Lord our God did visit us with assurances that he would deliver us; yea, insomuch that he did speak peace to our souls, and did grant unto us great faith, and did cause us that we should hope for our deliverance in him." - Alma 58:11*

thinking one of my favorite scriptures that I had pressed to memory came to mind. "Know ye not that ye are in the hands of God? Know ye not that God has all power?" (Mormon 5:23) Knowing I was in God's hands and knowing that he has all power how could I fear or fell forsaken?

To be this pillar of strength and faith for my son would have been impossible minutes earlier. I felt "troubled on every side, yet not distressed...perplexed, but not in despair; Persecuted, but not forsaken; cast down but not destroyed" (2 Corinthians 4:8-9).

After Parker finally arrived and the doctors had left the room, we were able to call our children living out of state and

allow them to join with us over speaker phone as we knelt for a family prayer on behalf of Lexi. From the deepest and most tender part of my soul, I plead to God as the prayer was offered that He would hear a mother's plea on behalf of her daughter and heal Lexi just as the Savior had raised Lazarus from the dead. Every thought and word spoken was directed heavenward seeking a divine answer.

Although it had felt much longer, it had only been just over an hour since we received the call to come to the hospital. I felt myself standing on a small foothill, looking ahead to a steep mountain of adversity. Little did I know how rugged the rest of the journey to the peak would be and how long it would take to discover if God would allow a miracle to happen on Lexi's behalf. But I could feel the wind at my back, pushing me upwards on the rocky incline and knew there would be much more soul stretching in the hours and days ahead. As Job, I knew that God could "do every *thing*" (Job 42:2), "for the eyes of the Lord *are* over the righteous and his ears *are open* unto their prayers" (1 Peter 3:12).

CHAPTER FOUR

THE MIRACLE OF A GRATEFUL HEART

"In everything give thanks." - 1 Thess. 5:18

After our family prayer, I suggested that each of us individually kneel down and say a silent prayer of gratitude for our many blessings. I believe that there is great power in gratitude prayers. While I prayed, I pondered on the many instances where Lexi had shown thanksgiving. Hers was a soul overflowing with appreciation, especially when it came to God's creations. I wistfully reflected on the last evening she was at home.

"Mom, did you see the sunset?" Lexi asked breathlessly as she came running in the house to make sure I didn't miss it. "It's spectacular!" she said in earnestness, flashing a smile at me.

I hurried to the window and saw the most brilliant reds and oranges painting the canvas of the sky in a fiery display.

I loved that about Lexi: she was always on the lookout for goodness. As the sun receded

> *"It is not happy people who are thankful. It is thankful people who are happy." - Author Unknown*

behind the mountain, the wave of colors still lingered as if accidentally left behind before vanishing in the sky. Lexi was spell bound, like it was the first time she'd seen the splendor of the setting sun. She never lost her enthusiasm for the nightly event. Each new sunset became her favorite.

Lexi's gratitude was contagious because she was always happy. My mind continued to sift through the sweet memories as image after image sprang to my mind.

One cool and crisp fall morning, when the trees were sporting new autumn colors of red and yellow, Lexi couldn't resist  the temptation of calling out to her brothers to come help as she ran to grab a rake. Our yard was a sea of leaves, and she couldn't believe her good fortune. Within an hour I heard her contagious laugh and hurried outside to join in the festivities. I knew whatever they had been up to would prove to be fun. There was always a spontaneous energy about her.

Just under the big globe willow tree was a massive pile of leaves they had worked hard to create. I stepped outside just in time to see Lexi leaning forward out of the tree, squinting up at the sun before she sailed out of the safety of its branches into the enormous mountain of crusty brown and orange leaves gleaming in the sunlight. Laughing hysterically, leaves poking from her hair, she threw up a handful of leaves in the air before calling out to Parker to jump.

I wanted to open a door where time stood still and return to those carefree days, but the sniffles from family members brought my thoughts back to reality, and the pain pierced through me once again. I needed to focus, to remember her goodness, to let the Lord know I was thankful for what was now 18 very short years.  Glancing up, I saw a few of my children getting up off their knees, but I couldn't stop praying just yet. I retreated back into my thoughts.

> *"Cease not to give thanks." - Eph. 1:16*

Lexi's own gratitude was evident at an early age. A treasured memory to me occurred when she was just seven

years old. She had lost a tooth and was so excited for the Tooth
Fairy to come. I assumed it was to get money.

That night, when the last of
daylight had faded away, I crept into her
room and knelt by her bed to put some
coins under her pillow. Much to my
surprise, I found a sweet note addressed
to the tooth fairy, some coins, and a
miniature tea set. In the note she
thanked the Tooth Fairy for being so
kind to all the boys and girls in the world by giving them
money for their teeth. She continued by explaining that she
knew she must be tired, so the tea set was for her to relax and
take a break. Then she wrote that she didn't want any money
for her tooth, but instead wanted to give the Tooth Fairy money
so she would not have to work as hard. Lexi had very little
money at that age and had given every last coin to the tooth
fairy.

Then another recollection came so vividly, I felt I could
reach out and touch it as it happened on my mind. It was a
warm spring day when dark gray clouds gathered in the sky,
releasing a sudden shower. The downpour pelted our roof,
startling everyone inside. Not one to feel cooped
up, Lexi squealed with delight as she scampered out the door,
barefoot, with the rest of her siblings, not hesitating a moment.

Forming a line, they zigzagged, jumped, and twirled - following the leader of the pack's every move. Rain trickled down their faces as they stomped in fresh pools of water, relishing every second of the downpour. A smile stole across Lexi's face. She saw every kind of storm as a blessing in disguise. She seemed just as grateful for the rain as the light now filtering through the clouds. I wished I could go back in time - if just for a day - to feel of her love and gratitude.

How could I not be thankful for the time I had with her? I was a better person in her presence because she made me feel of worth. She never expected anything, even on her birthday. In fact, she would specifically ask me not to give her a present. And no matter how small the gift or gesture, her appreciation knew no bounds.

I would invariably find a note on my pillow when we came home from a vacation thanking me for the fun trip. Even though our trips weren't exotic, like a few of her friends had been, she never compared the two or felt slighted that we couldn't spend as much on them. Her considerations continued to be on being a giver. She had a warmth about her that made others feel comfortable. Neighbors and friends were surprised to find notes in their mail box thanking them for service they had given to her or to others.

My heart continued to swell while I pondered on Lexi's spirit. Yet, soon I was pulled away from my wistful musings and reluctantly got up off my knees.

Looking back on this experience as we knelt as a family, I realize that saying a prayer of thanks wouldn't have entered my mind at a time like this if it wasn't for a tender mercy given to me a month before the accident. While I was saying my nightly prayer, I had the distinct impression to start speaking only gratitude prayers. Morning and evening, individual and family petitions became communion with God to acknowledge everything He had given me.

At first, when I began the practice of only thanking God for the blessings I'd received, it was hard not to sneak in a favor that was desperately

> "I thank my God always on your behalf." - 1 Cor. 1:4

needed. It was particularly difficult not to ask the Lord to help my children. After all, one daughter was struggling to get pregnant, and a son was in need of a job. However, in time I grew in spiritual wisdom and I no longer struggled to only pray

34

with thanksgiving. I felt calm and peaceful, in contrast to prayers of pleading and desperation, and I began to find that I was more receptive to the whisperings of the Holy Spirit when I would only give prayers of appreciation.

Also, in time I came to understand that gratitude brought benefits to my life that I was not fully aware of until later.

Instead of asking for my daughter to get pregnant, I learned to say thank you for a beautiful daughter who remains faithful and steadfast despite not being able to bear a child at this time. And I was able to give thanks for a son who trusts in God's plan for him despite not finding a job. It changed my whole perspective as I prayed with thanksgiving. I began to see God's grace unfold in my life, instead of seeing petitions unanswered. Developing this habit before the accident made it second nature to give a prayer of gratitude at the hospital.

The scriptures teach, "Verily I say unto you my friends, fear not, let your hearts be comforted; yea, rejoice evermore, and in everything give thanks . . . for your prayers have entered into the ears of the Lord..." And then this amazing promise is given: ". . . all things wherewith you have been afflicted shall work together for your good" (D&C 98:1-3).

While each member of the family spent some time on his or her knees thanking Heavenly Father for blessings, a feeling of love and humility came over all of us, and we knew that the Lord was in charge. After those tender moments of expressing gratitude to our Father in Heaven, I felt a greater outpouring of the spirit.

> *"Lord I will praise thee forever; yea my soul will rejoice in thee, my God and the rock of my salvation." - 2 Nephi 4: 30*

Later, as we had the opportunity of telling Lexi's story many times and on one occasion while being interviewed, I was felt impressed to include this experience. I hoped that others might be inspired to express more appreciation in their prayers. As I was telling a reporter our experience, she stopped me to ask what a gratitude prayer was. As I explained what kind of prayer that would entail, she was incredulous. She didn't believe that anyone could give a prayer of gratitude while their daughter lay lifeless in the emergency room. And with all things considered, she assumed her readers would not believe me either.

She asked, "What in the world did you pray for at that difficult moment in time?"

I explained that I thanked my Father in Heaven for the 18 years that he'd allowed me to have with my daughter, particularly for her goodness, for her love for the Lord, for her bright and happy spirit, and for her light. I likewise thanked him for my other children, as well as for their good lives that

reflected God's kindness to everyone they met. I thanked Him for my Savior, who is the great Healer, for His atoning sacrifice, and for His anguish in Gethsemane that allowed Him to understand my suffering at that very minute. In short, I told the reporter, I knew that there was more power in gratitude prayers despite what most people may believe.

Among many other reasons, I believe one reason Lexi is still here with us today is because God blesses those who recognize his kindness and who focus on what others have done for them and not solely on their own selfish desires. He wanted to teach me a lesson, and for that I will always be thankful. Acknowledging God's hand in my life has changed me.

One of my favorite people in the Book of Mormon is Captain Moroni. We are told that "if all men had been, and were, and ever would be like unto Moroni, behold, the very powers of hell would have been shaken forever." What was he like? One important characteristic is that he was "a man whose heart did swell with thanksgiving to his God, for the many privileges and blessings which he bestowed upon his people;" (Alma 48:17, 12). Perhaps it was Moroni's ability to give thanks that allowed him to have such spiritual power.

Another account I love is that of the prophet Daniel in the Old Testament. In his day, a decree went forth throughout the kingdom stating that no one was

> *"It is easy to be grateful for things when life seems to be going well... Could I suggest that we see gratitude as a disposition, a way of life that stands independent of our current situation? In other words, I'm suggesting that instead of being 'thankful for things' we focus on being 'thankful in our circumstances' - whatever they may be." - Dieter F. Uchtdorf, "Grateful in Any Circumstances," Ensign, May 2014, (two months after Lexi's accident)*

permitted to pray or they would be killed. After learning of this law, Daniel "went into his house; and his windows being open . . . he kneeled upon his knees three times a day, and prayed, and gave *thanks* before his God, as he did aforetime" (Daniel 6:10, emphasis added).

Because he disobeyed the King's command, he was taken to the lion's den to be killed. But Daniel explains, "God hath sent his angel, and hath shut the lions' mouths, that they have not hurt me" (Daniel 6:22). Can we not attribute Daniel's miraculous escape from the lion's den to the prayers of gratitude he had offered up? Fasting was also part of this miracle (and we will soon see it would also be a part of Lexi's miracle), as the scriptures explain that after they brought Daniel and cast him into the den of lions, "Then the king went to his palace, and passed the night fasting" (Daniel 6:18).

In the hospital, just after we had finished our gratitude prayers, an employee came in to tell us they had seen a "hint of life" in Lexi, and they were going to move her upstairs to the Intensive Care Unit (ICU). What a powerful testimony to our family of the power of prayer! It was immediately after we finished our petitions that her chance of survival went from almost zero percent to one percent. We realized later that if we had not offered those prayers, we don't believe that she would still be with us now.

As we have looked back on this experience, we stand in awe at how quickly the Lord answered our pleadings for Lexi. Our testimony in the power of prayer increased greatly-- especially in gratitude prayers. God does hear us. He wants to bless us and will pour out as many blessings upon our heads as we are ready to accept. He is waiting for us to come to Him for help.

The beginning of this miracle had commenced and we were literal witnesses of God's power to heal and change an outcome that seemed to have already been decided by doctors and science. We learned for ourselves that to such an extent that we "seek the Lord God…with all [our] heart and all [our] soul…and with [our] whole desire, he [is] found of [us] (2 Chronicles 15:12, 15).

CHAPTER FIVE

THE MIRACLE OF CHRIST'S
HEALING POWER OF FORGIVENESS

"And be ye kind one to another, tenderhearted, forgiving one another, even as God for Christ's sake hath forgiven you?" - Ephesians 4:32

When we walked into the hallway to go upstairs to the ICU, I saw a group of Lexi's friends huddled together in the corridor, somber and full of anxiety. Word had spread rapidly on social media of Lexi's accident, and they had rushed directly over to the hospital, waiting desperately for any information on her status.

I wanted to encircle my arms around them and console them. I could see the grief and despair in their faces. But, just then, the glass doors slid open and an EMT came walking in the building carrying Lexi's backpack and the two broken pieces of her longboard. My heart quickened with dread. Seeing her damaged longboard pierced my soul and made me physically ill at a time when I didn't think my pain could grow any worse. Yet, somehow it did.

I abruptly looked the other way and stared silently at the wall to avoid looking at her personal possessions. I tried to drown out the image that had filled my mind, perceiving I would collapse if I gave into my feelings. In a daze, I followed the assistant upstairs, where we were led to a waiting area on the floor of the ICU.

During this time, my son McKay and my daughter-in-law Makana, drove to the scene of the accident in hopes of finding the driver of the car that hit Lexi to make sure that he was OK. I had been caught off guard when one the first things McKay said to me after we had seen Lexi's lifeless body was that our family needed to go check on the driver. The world had just come crashing down on us, and, yet, he was able to look beyond our harsh surroundings to someone else's plight.

I had still been in shock, trying to awake from my awful nightmare and found it extraordinary that he had the presence of mind to think of the driver at that horrifying

"...and forgiving one another...even as Christ forgave you, so also do ye." - Cor. 3:13

moment. Each of us knew the torment the driver must have been going through upon realizing that he might have killed someone and wanted to make sure he was OK. All I could muster was a nod of my head, but inside I was pleased that the driver had not been forgotten in his time of need.

Regrettably he had left by the time my son and his wife got there. And the driver told us later that he was actually worried that we would try to find him and was relieved that he was allowed to leave the scene before we got there.

As I reflected on this experience later, I realized that McKay and Makana's reaction was very much like the prophet Alma in the Book of Mormon. Alma went to the city of Ammonihah to preach the gospel, but to no avail, as the people "reviled him, and spit upon him, and caused that he should be cast out of their city" (Alma 8:13). Upon leaving the city and "being weighed down with sorrow…because of [their] wickedness…an angel of the Lord appeared unto him saying…return to the city" (Alma 8:14, 16).

I love Alma's response. He doesn't complain and say it was a hard thing that he was required to do, but, instead, the record states that "he returned speedily" (Alma 8:13-18). He had full confidence God was in charge, and his gait showed a man that was joyful to have the opportunity to return to teach.

That is exactly the reaction of my son and daughter-in-law as we received the horrible news that our precious Lexi had no chance of survival. They "speedily" rushed back to the scene of the accident to find the driver and to console him. They knew instinctively to love and to forgive, as their angel

43

came in the form of the Holy Ghost. They didn't put limits on their compassion by making excuses or holding a grudge until the offending party apologized.

They could have easily have said in their hearts that forgiveness was all well and good, but just not in this situation because it involved their sister who they loved and.admired. Was our family really supposed to forgive the person who might have killed Lexi?

Gratefully, our entire family felt the same way, to let the driver know of our love and to follow the scriptural admonition, "I, the Lord, will forgive whom I will forgive, but of you it is required to forgive all men" (D&C 64:10).

Is this not a greater miracle? The ability to forgive and to love unconditionally? Do we sometimes mistakenly believe that the offending party needs to come to us and ask for forgiveness before we can forgive them? Forgiveness brings healing--both to those who are forgiven and also to those who absolve them of their guilt, thus bringing respite to both.

We sat and prayed silently in the waiting room while they were stitching up Lexi's face in the ICU. I knew that I couldn't supplicate the Lord with so great a petition unless I was kneeling. I felt I needed to give the God of this universe, He who

> "Casting all your care upon him for he careth for you."
> - 1 Peter 5:7

gives sight to the blind and healing to the lame and the breath of life to my daughter, my utmost respect and devotion. It might seem like a small thing, but, to me, I knew of no other way to approach a Being that could restore life to the dead than to kneel, even though it meant doing so in a very public place. With these thoughts in mind, I found a corner of the waiting room and knelt in prayer. I pleaded with God to know His will for Lexi. Would my heart be strong enough to bear the coming test? I needed to "come boldly unto the throne of grace…to help [me in this] time of need" (Hebrews 4:16).

As I continued to pray in my heart, my siblings arrived and gave me support with expressions of love and faith. My

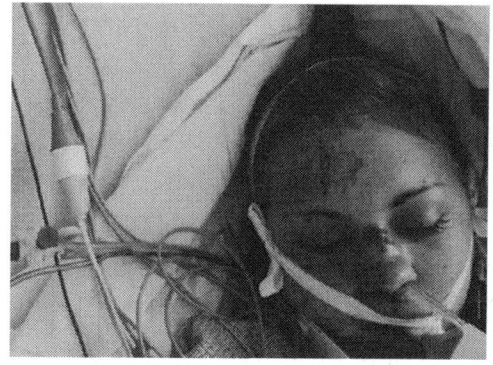

brother told me of his own intercessory prayer on my behalf. He explained to the Lord that I was a good and faithful woman of God and that I was worthy to have my petitions for my daughter answered. Oh, how those words touched me and gave me courage! To know that I had nothing to hide, no great sins that would keep me from asking for God's healing touch to renew Lexi's body and bring her back whole and well was priceless. I also knew of my brother's great faith and felt that if anyone could pray for Heaven's help in my behalf, he could. My son Tanner similarly whispered comfort, as he bore his testimony to me. I needed his testimony, as it was a reminder to me that the Redeemer is the Giver of Life.

When they had finished stitching up Lexi's face, a nurse's voice jarred my mind back to the present as she asked me and my husband to follow her to Lexi's room. As I stood up to go, I could barely move my feet one in front of the other. My body seemed to be shutting down, and my legs refused to obey me. It was as if I was walking through quick sand.

Shuffling down the corridor, we finally reached her room. We were only allowed to stay for a couple of minutes, however, before we were ushered again into the waiting room. As the doors swung open wide, I tried again to move my legs but couldn't. I was immobilized, too weak to support myself. It was a surreal experience.

Without saying a word, my brothers knew instinctively that I needed aid and hurried to my side. Taking each arm, they assisted me to a nearby chair where I subsequently collapsed. Seeing what bad shape I was in, they asked if I would like a blessing. My son Tanner offered to be the mouthpiece for God.

"Certainly I will be with thee," (Exodus 3:12) is the message that I felt as Tanner spoke words from our Father in Heaven. Not just that God would be with me, which would be powerful in and of itself, but God added the word *certainly* to ensure there would be no confusion about His loyalty. He would be the source of my strength. It was a beautiful blessing and gave me the added fortitude that my heart and spirit needed to get through what would be a long and sleepless night.

Would God, the God of Miracles, choose in His great knowledge and wisdom to make Lexi whole? I was haunted by the unknown. And I had no idea of the intense and gut-wrenching struggle still ahead of me. I would need to reach to the very ends of my soul to know what God's desire for our family would be, but one thing I did know was that *He* could give us a miracle.

I gathered all the physical strength I could muster after my husband and I were summoned once again to go back into Lexi's room. As we entered, a nurse was incensed that we had come in the wrong door from the waiting area and immediately started to scold us. I stood in stunned silence at her rebuke, while the Physician's Assistant promptly told her that he was to blame, as he had asked us to follow him. But, the nurse gave me a smoldering look and with self-righteous indignation continued to get after us: "You shouldn't have gone this way," she said coldly.

I was totally caught off guard. It had only been a few hours since Lexi's accident. I was still in severe shock and filled with overwhelming heartache. Yet we were getting rebuked for the most trivial of sins. The conversation wasn't worth engaging in, but I couldn't take her flippant attitude anymore and said calmly but firmly, "Seriously? You are getting after me for going in the wrong door while my daughter is lying here in front of you, near death?"

She squirmed a little at my temperate rebuke, but it only made her dig in her heels more and repeat like a drill sergeant the importance of going through the right door. I blew out a breath in exasperation. I was dumbfounded at the lack of compassion she had for us.

As the PA left the room, I followed after him and asked him if he could get us a new nurse. I told him that I knew that the only way that Lexi would be healed is by angels, but they would not come in a room filled with contention. I was surprised by my own words. I had never thought about asking for angels to help me because I had the Holy Ghost to guide and direct me. Yet, the impression had come forcefully to my mind. It was absolutely clear to me that angels would be invaluable for her survival.

The PA explained to me that this nurse was one of the best on the floor and that I wouldn't want to switch her. Upon hearing this I realized that her expertise would also be an essential part in Lexi's survival. I needed to turn this unpleasant experience into a good one, to become her friend in order to have Heaven's help. So I returned to the room with an open heart and inquired about her family and interests, despite my own grief. The corners of her mouth softened, and, although she never apologized, it wasn't long until the room was filled with warmth. With the previous tension gone, I realized I had survived this encounter. Forgiving the nurse now freed me to focus on Lexi.

It was a harsh reality to learn that despite the grief I was experiencing that others would add to my cloud of despair instead of looking for ways to take my

> *"For what glory is it, if, when ye be buffeted for your faults, ye shall take it patiently? but if, when ye do well, and suffer for it, ye take it patiently, this is acceptable with God." - 1 Peter 2:20*

pain away. I wondered how many times I had made this same mistake by letting pride get in the way of charity just to prove a point or allowing the letter of the law distract me from things that matter most.

I was able to reach out to this nurse in kindness, when I saw her as a child of God. I tried to envision what she might be going through in her own life. Did she have pressing problems of her own that might have caused her to lash out at me? Recognizing these other possibilities, her jarring words no longer held their sting.

I have always delighted reading the final part of the story of Joseph who had been sold into slavery by his brothers. Because of a famine in all the land, Joseph's brothers had traveled to Egypt to buy grain. However they had no idea that the person that they were negotiating with was their brother. I become emotional each time I read the account of Joseph when he reveals himself to his brothers, reassuring them of his love and forgiveness. He declares, "Be not

49

grieved, nor angry with yourselves, that ye sold me hither: for God did send me before you to preserve life." (Gen. 45:5) Joseph showed compassion and tenderness, instead of exacting revenge, and we love him for it. As I began to show the nurse charity, my heart changed and I felt only love for her. Just as I knew that forgiving the nurse and the driver was paramount to having the faith needed for a miracle, so it is in our daily walk of life. God's power will be magnified fourfold as we quickly forgive.

CHAPTER SIX

THE MIRACLE OF THE PRIESTHOOD

"Behold, I will lead thee by my hand, and I will take thee, to put upon thee my name, even the Priesthood of thy father, and my power shall be over thee." - Abraham 1: 18

Shortly after my husband, Doug, and I were permitted to come back into Lexi's room, they allowed the rest of the family to do so as well. Usually they don't allow large groups to congregate in the ICU, but I'm sure they allowed all of us to be there together that night because they didn't believe she would live until morning.

Clutching forcefully to the rail of her bed with one hand, while gripping fiercely to my daughter-in-law Makana's hand with the other, brought momentary relief. Yet inside me I could feel a volcano of pain erupting again. I stared expressionless at Lexi but continued to squeeze tighter and tighter, hoping the crush of my hands could alleviate my anguish.

As I stared at her, I knew she could come through this. She had always been tough and was such a fighter. I thought back to a tennis match I had eagerly come to watch. Lex was a natural—agile and quick, her skin bronzed from hours playing on the court. She was on fire, rocketing volleys with perfect timing as she lobbed over the net.

The first time she had picked up a tennis racket, she could hit with her back hand with the same precision and power as her right, something rarely seen. But she was still very motivated to practice, setting high goals for herself. When the sun peeked over the mountain, she was up, riding her bike to the courts. In the evening, she would continue to develop her stroke and top spin by hammering the ball against our garage door hundreds of times, every stroke deliberate, until her arm became sore. The throbbing pain in her elbow would sometimes become so excruciating, she couldn't play.

Her serve was near perfection—one of the best in the state--the toss high and forward. Then--wham!--another precise placement, making her opponent scramble for the ball or, more often, resulting in another ace. It wasn't unusual for Lexi to even beat some of the boys' varsity team players. She was a fierce competitor and would dart across the court, diving for a ball and scraping her elbows and knees in the process, sacrificing her body for a point.

The beeping of the machine startled me. I glanced up, and across from me stood my son Tanner. Instantly, I felt the impression that Lexi was to have another priesthood blessing, although she had already been given a one in the ER. I knew that the sacred healing power of the priesthood, the power of God, was another aspect of what was needed to make Lexi whole.

> "...the rights of the priesthood are inseparably connected with the powers of heaven..."
> - D&C 121:36

I had a great deal of faith in each of the men in my family to receive inspiration to know the mind and will of God and to have the heavens opened to them. I had read stories in the scriptures and knew personally of the miracles that can and do occur as men speak what God would say if He were here on earth. Would God through the worthy priesthood holders in our family be inspired to bless Lexi to be made whole?

Tanner describes his feelings as he gave Lexi her second priesthood blessing in this way:

"On the night of the accident I had the strong impression that I needed to give Lexi a blessing of healing. However, I knew that I was lacking the faith necessary to do it. I felt just as the father with the child possessed by the evil spirit in Mark 9:23-24: "Jesus said unto him, If thou canst believe, all things are possible to him that believeth. And straightway the father of the child cried out, and said with tears, Lord, I believe; help thou mine unbelief."I also felt like Jairus in Mark 5: "And, behold, there cometh one of the rulers of the synagogue, Jairus by name; and when he saw him, he fell at his feet, And besought him greatly, saying, My little daughter lieth at the point of death: *I pray thee*, come and lay thy hands on her, that she may be healed; and she shall live. . . While he yet spake, there came from the ruler of the synagogue's house certain which said, Thy daughter is dead: why troublest thou the Master any further? As soon as Jesus heard the word that was spoken, he saith unto the ruler of the synagogue, Be not afraid, only believe" (22-23, 35-36).

Just like this father, I pleaded with the Lord to help me have the faith to believe that a miracle could come forth. As I prayed, I felt the Lord strengthening me so I, too, could believe. And although I was given the strength to believe, I still had to act, and that was the hardest part.

When we finally got to see Lexi, a wave of emotion and fear overcame me as I saw what state she was in. But the Lord did not fail me; He truly lifted me and strengthened my faith at a time when I needed to have the courage to give my sister a blessing of healing.

As I laid my hands upon her head, I felt such confidence in the Lord through the Spirit that she would be healed. As I spoke, the words that came were not my own but were the words of God. These words, "be not unbelieving, but only believe," and "through the Atonement of Jesus Christ she will be healed," still ring in my ears today and bring me great comfort and peace. At that moment I knew without a doubt that she would be healed through Him. The sacredness of the blessing cannot fully be expressed - but, in that moment, I knew without a doubt that the power of Christ was real.

I have pondered on those words, "through the Atonement of Jesus Christ she will be healed," many times. I knew that this healing process she would go through would be long and difficult, just like it is in our lives at times. But I also know that, just like Lexi, we can be healed not only physically but spiritually through Him as well. The power of the priesthood is real! I know that Christ lives - there is no doubt in my mind. I testify of His power and love. I love Him; He is my Savior and King, and through Him we can all be healed."

This priesthood blessing was a direct answer to our family that God would heal Lexi if we exhibited enough faith in Him so that He could accomplish His grand design in our family's behalf.

My son Tanner continues:

"Since day one of Lexi's accident, my mom had the impression from the Holy Ghost that Lexi would need a priesthood blessing every day to continue to progress. On top of that, my mom also made sure we were always wearing a white shirt and tie, as it symbolizes cleanliness and priesthood power. I watched as my brothers, father, and brother-in-laws each prepared through fasting and prayer to give Lexi beautiful, inspired blessings.

We truly saw the huge impact it had on Lexi and her progress when we gave her a blessing. Each time she was given a blessing, the room was immediately filled with the Spirit, and we felt the presence of angels in the room, strengthening her. Not only did Lexi start to heal, but our own faith was subsequently strengthened as we prepared for these blessings. Each blessing was an added witness that she would be made whole and restored to her health completely.

A few times when we didn't give her a blessing, there was a noticeable difference, as Lexi struggled a lot more in her progress. As a result, my mom would hurry and call one of the priesthood holders in the family to come in and give her a blessing, and then she would start to improve again.

Through priesthood blessings, we have heard the voice of God and have felt His power and ability to heal Lexi. We know that God is perfectly aware of the situations we are in and that He loves each of His children. How grateful we are for a loving Heavenly Father who has provided us with the Book of Mormon to bring us knowledge of His plan for us and comfort in our time of need."

Although only one blessing is needed after an accident or illness, as Tanner mentioned, I had a strong impression that Lexi needed to receive a blessing every day. A couple of family members reminded me that this wasn't necessary, but I couldn't deny the spiritual prompting I felt to do this. In fact as soon as my husband and sons walked in Lexi's room wearing their white shirts and ties, I felt a power overshadow me, much like the people in Peter's day felt when he walked the streets.

Because of Peter's extraordinary faith and exact obedience, the believing brought the sick into the streets on beds "that at least the shadow of Peter passing by might overshadow some of them…and they were healed every one" (Acts 5:15-16).

There cannot be power given from heaven unless mortal men are clean, worthy, ready, and righteous, as Peter was, so that God can speak through them. This is because "the powers of heaven cannot be controlled nor handled only upon the principles of righteousness" (D&C 121:36).

I was grateful to know I could call on any priesthood holder in my family and know they were pure and prepared in every way spiritually to use the gift given to them. They had taken to heart the words of Joshua when he said, "Sanctify yourselves: for to morrow the Lord will do wonders among you" (Joshua 3:5). We never know when our faith will be needed, so we should always be watchful, prayerful, and remember to "Awake! and arise from the dust" (2 Nephi1:14).

CHAPTER SEVEN

THE MIRACLE TO KNOW THE WILL OF GOD

"I have trodden the wine press alone; and of the people there was none with me. . . I looked, and there was none to help; and I wondered that there was none to uphold." - Isaiah 63:3, 5

The night of Lexi's accident was the longest night of my life. I was heartbroken and devastated, staggering under a load of grief. Even though I had been reminded and knew deep within my heart that God could perform a miracle--and that Tanner, standing in as God's spokesman, had pronounced a blessing on her head that she would be healed--I had not received that witness from the Holy Ghost myself.

Looking back, I believe that the Lord had some things to teach me about suffering and about faith. I knew of Tanner's faith, and it had strengthened mine. But I also knew this blessing could not be realized without absolute faith on our family's part during this dark and terrible hour. Could we walk the bitter path of discipleship? I was shaken to the very core of my being, realizing that Lexi could be taken away from me. More than anything else, I needed to know God's will for myself.

There was a clock above Lexi's bed I looked at frequently, praying for the hours to go by quickly, so that the nightmare would end and I could take my daughter home. Instead, time seemed to stand still, as the night dragged on and on. While I sat by her bed, holding her hand between mine, the grief and suffering were unbearable. I decided that I would not look at the clock again until I knew that an hour had gone by. When what seemed like an eternity had passed, I eagerly looked up at the clock, knowing that I had erased away some dreadful moments of time. To my dismay, only two minutes had gone by! I couldn't understand how that could be possible. I knew that I had sat there for at least two hours. I said to myself, "Is it possible that the clock is wrong? How am I going to make it through this night filled with so much anguish?"

The Lord's promise to us is "I will not leave you comfortless," yet I felt no comfort (John 14:18). He said, "...peace I give unto you," yet I felt no peace (John 14:27). I'd never prayed, suffered, and struggled with more intensity in my life. When would the sun appear ending the agony of the night? It was as if the Lord was lengthening the time in order that I might more fully understand, in a small way, His own suffering. I closed my eyes and said another silent prayer, letting a pained groan escape. I breathed deeply, every second excruciating to live through.

Finally the morning did come, but it did not bring the relief I was expecting. That day passed by just as slowly, as I "did cry mightily to God; yea, even all the day long did [I]

> *"Hath God forgotten to be gracious? Hath he in anger shut up his tender mercies?" - Psalm 77:9*

cry unto [my] God that he would deliver [me] out of [my] afflictions" (Mosiah 21:14).

As I sat by Lexi's bed hour after hour, holding her hand, feeling her spirit, I had a lot of time to reflect. One thing I realized immediately was that the Lord was in this experience before the accident even happened. As I explained in the first chapter, I was prompted to say only gratitude prayers a month before the accident happened. However, that is not the only way that he prepared me personally.

As the gospel doctrine teacher[10] of my congregation, I had been preparing the lesson on Abraham sacrificing his son Isaac the morning before Lexi was hit. As I studied for the lesson, I was prompted to listen to a podcast on the Mormon Channel called "Enduring It Well." I had discovered this series

---

[10]Someone who teaches the adult Sunday school class in our church

for the first time when I had been looking for a modern day example of Abraham and Isaac.

I clicked on the podcast and listened to a story about a family that had lost a child to a disease. I was deeply touched by their faith. I was mesmerized as I listened to how they dealt with their shock, sorrow, and gloom by turning to the Savior. They related how they coped with their new reality, their sorrow, and the dramatic change in their lives by trusting in God's plan for them and their loved one.

I continued to listen to story after story on this station while I did chores around the house, fighting my emotions because of the unbelievable, heart-wrenching stories.

Deep within my soul, I desired to be like these individuals and families. Could I also not waver, no matter the amount of adversity thrown my way? In my time of "trouble" could I "[turn] unto the Lord God of Israel, and [seek] Him," knowing "He [would be] found"? (2 Chronicles 15:4).

These stories were so inspiring that I even called two of my daughters living out of state to relate to them what I had learned. I found it incredible that these families who had lost loved ones and individuals that had either lost limbs or had become paralyzed could feel such peace and understanding. But more than anything, I sorrowed for their pain and their loss. I felt sure that a death or a similar tragedy would not

> *"No matter how serious the trial, how deep the distress, how great the affliction, [God] will never desert us. He never has, and He never will. He cannot do it. It is not His character [to do so]. He is an unchangeable being; the same yesterday, the same today, and He will be the same throughout the eternal ages to come. We have found that God. We have made Him our friend, by obeying His Gospel; and He will stand by us. We may pass through the fiery furnace; we may pass through deep waters; but we shall not be consumed nor overwhelmed. We shall emerge from all these trials and difficulties the better and purer for them, if we only trust in our God and keep His commandments." - George Q. Cannon("Freedom of the saints, "In Collected Discourses, comp. Brian H. Stuy, 5 vols. [1987-92], 2:185)*

happen to me because I could barely even listen to the heartbreaking stories of total strangers. They had been where most of us have never gone and hope never to go. I figured God knew me well enough to know I could not handle a sorrow of such magnitude. He knew what I could bear.

A specific idea mentioned in the podcast stood out to me: it was one thing to say you will have faith when something bad happens to you, but it is another thing all together to actually live through and experience a trial firsthand. Only then will you know whether or not your faith is strong enough not to waver. How much faith do you really possess?

Each person interviewed on the series reiterated the point that faith in God really means trusting God. Can you trust that God knows what is best for you even though you don't like the outcome? Trust was the key to unwavering faith that I would teach about on Sunday, or so I thought.

I continued to listen to these real-life examples to help me better prepare me for my lesson on Sunday, not realizing that I would never teach that lesson. Instead I would be called upon to *live* that lesson. Would I be strong enough to apply those principles in my own life?

I soon found that what these families said was absolutely true. My faith was in need of being strengthened tenfold. As the shock, the pain, the absolute trauma of the experience seemed too much to bear, one of the first things that came to my mind was the words of these individuals on the podcast series: "Faith means trusting the Lord." It was one of the many loving mercies given to me, as I was reminded that God knew me and that I must trust in what *His* plan for me would be. I had no need to be afraid, for God was "with [me] to deliver [me]" (Jeremiah 1:8). I let those words sink in.

I knew Jesus had opened the eyes of the blind and healed the sick. He could also heal Lexi. And I knew He could carry me through this experience because He had already borne my anguish and despair. I wanted Him to silence my aching heart. I knew His was the only well I could drink from. I tried to keep that thought in the forefront of my mind. Now was the time to prove that my faith was unwavering, that I *would* trust God no matter the outcome.

But still I needed to know what the Lord's desire was for Lexi. Was it God's will that her life be extended? I breathed in deeply, continuing to reach Heavenward with my thoughts and prayers. I knew, as the angel, that nothing is "too hard for the Lord" (Genesis 18:14).

The topic of my upcoming lesson was one of the first things I thought of when I got to the hospital. I realized my heart and mind had been prepared as I pondered about doing all that the Lord might ask of me. Could I also be like Abraham, as I climbed my mountain, and say with absolute faith, "Thy will be done," even if it required giving up Lexi? I cried out silently to God, "I know you were preparing me, but I don't want to be prepared. I cannot do this." I knew without a doubt God had done all he could to fortify me, but I didn't believe I was strong enough for the enormity of this adversity.

As the hours went by, I continued to think about Abraham. I thought about how Isaac had been spared from the knife of death. Would my daughter be saved? Would there be a ram in the thicket for me? Part of me thought that she might be shielded and that the Lord was reminding me by this lesson that He could do all things, as He did for Abraham. The other side of me thought that because I knew the ending to the story, there would be no need for faith on my behalf if she were shown mercy too. I would need to be obedient as Abraham and not expect her to live.

Never before in my life have I hungered and thirsted to "be filled with the Holy Ghost" (3 Nephi 12:6) so that I could know the mind and will of the Lord. I desperately wanted to know what to ask for through personal revelation. I yearned and sought diligently for that truth to enlighten and empower my mind. I didn't want to ask amiss. I knew trials were part of mortality but so was God's love and mercy. The words I had read so often before came to my mind, "...yet will I not forget thee. Behold, I have graven thee upon the palms of my hands" (Isaiah 49:15-16).

I shared this story of Abraham, as well as my wrestle to know what to pray for, with my son JD. I confessed that maybe it wasn't God's will to spare Lexi. I wanted to make sure that as I prayed, I would only do what God would want.

After thinking about what I had said to him for a few hours, JD had a sudden flash of insight, and came back to the room. He looked at me in earnest.

"Mom," he said, "I've been thinking about Abraham. I know that Abraham was willing to be obedient to the Lord even to the sacrificing of his son Isaac, but..."

Then he hesitated, trying to form his thoughts the way he had heard them in his mind so that there would be no misunderstanding. He calmly continued, "I think that Abraham probably pleaded with the Lord to show mercy on his son as he traveled to Mount Moriah." His eyes stared deeply into my own, hoping that I would understand what he was trying to say to me. It was a stunning revelation.

His words hit my heart, and I immediately knew that what he said was true. I said, "So you are saying that you believe that Abraham pleaded for God to change his will?" I shifted my weight, looking away from his gaze, to ponder what he had just said to me and to let that concept sink in.

Pausing to collect my thoughts, I turned my eyes back to his. "You are exactly right," I said. "In my studies of Abraham, the journey to Mount Moriah would have taken Abraham three days...three *long* days," purposely drawing out the word long for emphasis.

There was a mutual understanding between me and JD of how truly excruciating those three days would have been for Abraham, now having gone through it ourselves. I continued thinking out loud: "As such, he had three days to plead with the Lord to have mercy on him."

I reached out and grabbed both of my son's hands and squeezed them before I wrapped my arms around him and hugged him fast, saying, "That is exactly what we are to do.

You have given me the additional courage and faith, and most importantly the knowledge to go to the Lord and ask Him to change His plan for Lexi, as He did for Isaac." For it was "By faith Abraham when he was tried, offered up Isaac;…his only begotten son. Accounting that God was able to raise him up, even from the dead." (Hebrews 11:17,19)

I was indecisive no longer. I knew like the prophet Nephi that "God [would] give me, if I ask[ed] not amiss" (2 Nephi 4:35). I turned my gaze back on Lexi and ever so lightly kissed her hand and laid my cheek on her arm. My love overflowed for her, for God, and for the knowledge that I might not have to let her go.

> *"And the Lord said,..I have prayed for thee, that thy faith fail not." - Luke 22:31-32*

Even if it had been God's intent to bring Lexi home to Him, we had the ability as a family and as a church and community to ask him to change those plans.

I was, nonetheless, hesitant, at first, to pray in that manner. Yet, I realized that trusting God is also about immediately taking action on the revelation given to us. Sometimes we trust and wait for God's will to unfold, but in this case I knew that I wasn't just to accept His will-- I was to ask for His will to be changed. How grateful I was that I was given these hours - which turned into days - to teach me to be bold in my prayers and to not allow my hope to falter.

During this time that I reflected on Abraham tediously walking for three days, pleading to the Lord to spare his son, my feelings for Abraham deepened, and I grew to love and understand him on a much more personal level. What a sweet tender mercy from the Lord to have been preparing to teach the story of Abraham and Isaac the week I would be facing a similar trial. God had literally borne me on eagle's wings, as he did for the children of Israel, and brought me to Him (Exodus 19:3-4). Now fortified with understanding and power beyond my own, I knew that the Lord would answer the righteous desires of my heart.

CHAPTER EIGHT

THE MIRACLE OF MIGHTY PRAYER

"But when they in their trouble did turn unto the Lord God of Israel, and sought him, he was found of them." - 2 Chronicles 15:4

The next morning we learned that Lexi's chances of living were slimmer than we originally had supposed. When the paramedics arrived she had to be resuscitated, which meant she had had some irreversible brain damage from the lack of oxygen to her brain during the time between the accidents and when resuscitation began. When she arrived at the hospital, she was assessed by doctors, who gave her no chance of survival. They weren't even going to take the time to stitch up her face and the organ donation team had been contacted and were already at the hospital before we got there.

To show how severe Lexi's injury was, the doctor also explained to us that her initial GCS (Glasgow Coma

Scale) score[11] when she first arrived at the hospital was 3, which is the lowest possible score (indicating a deep coma or death). The highest score, for a fully awake person, is 15. To reiterate how low Lexi's score really was, he pointed to a chair in the room and told us that the chair had the same functionality as someone with a GCS of a 3. I almost gasped at

the suggestion. I didn't know how to respond. His words bore down upon me.

I looked at Lexi. It was just too hard to believe that she had been as alive as a chair. I mean, this was Lexi, the girl who had just competed in a Tough Mudder race.

She had come home from that race caked in mud from head to toe, her body aching. After she had plunged into frigid water filled with ice chunks, hypothermia had set in, but she stubbornly had refused to quit. She was unconquerable, the only girl that

> *"God is always faithful...He never flees nor fails us." - Jeffrey R. Holland, "None Were With Him," Ensign, May 2009*

---

[11]A GCS (Glasgow Coma Scale) score is used to evaluate how conscious and responsive someone is after a traumatic brain injury and to help gauge the severity of the injury. A 3 is the lowest possible score.

day (that she knew of), to scale a skate boarding ramp: with clenched teeth, she sprinted up the side, as she miraculously caught her friend's hand, making it to the top. Her face flushed, gasping for air, she relished the challenge, not the slightest trace of fear in her body. And yet my heart knew that despite her fierce competitiveness, she had such a gentle heart. The memory lifted some of the sorrow, but only for an instant.

The doctors continued to emphasize that despite the fact that she had made it through the night, she still did not have much of a chance of survival. She already had swelling in her brain, and this swelling would only continue to get worse. It was just a matter of time to know how destructive the swelling would be.[12]

And because her injury was in the lower, central part of her brain, there was not much they could do to combat the swelling. In more external brain injuries they can remove the top of the skull to relieve the pressure on the brain, but this was not the case with Lexi. We knew of others that had suffered similar injuries who had died within a few days because of swelling in the brain.

We were told we had a long road ahead of us. After an initial injury to the brain, it can take up to two weeks to reach

[12]Swelling within the skull can directly damage brain cells or the pressure that can build within the skull can compress the brain and compromise its ability to function. (medicine net)

its maximum point of swelling. So, they indicated that it would be seven to ten days before they would know for sure if she would make it. There was never any doubt in my mind of God's miraculous power, but would it be His will to have her stay?

It was easy to pull back into my sanctuary of memories to help calm my troubled heart. Throughout the years, Lexi had had a glint of mischief in her bones and loved pranks. One

 particular morning, she awoke early to catch some ducks in a pond near our house. She chased and darted through the park after her feathered friends, but with no success. But in one wild moment, she gave it a final attempt - diving over a bush, arms outstretched, miraculously catching a straggler. Laughing and giggling, she caught her breath before setting the duck inside a box and into the trunk of her car.

Arriving at her high school, she discreetly let the duck out of its confinement and swooshed it inside the building to roam the halls, all while beaming from ear to ear that she had actually accomplished her mission. She had gone to all that trouble just to see the students' reaction. She could be who she was and was not afraid of what others might think. She liked to be different in a good way. I paused long enough in my thoughts for a fleeting smile.

Sitting by Lexi's bed, I tenderly planted a kiss on her arm. Daylight had vanished completely. It felt like two weeks had passed, and I had to remind myself that the accident happened only the night before. I was utterly exhausted both physically and spiritually. When my daughter, Kelsi, came in the room, I mentioned this to her. Seconds later my son, Parker, walked in the room and put forth the very same sentiment.

Knowing how the events of the past 24 hours had taken a toll on my body, my family insisted that I go to the family guest house[13] across the street from the hospital to get some sleep that night. Even though I didn't want to leave Lexi, I agreed to go in order to escape the nightmare I was living in, if only for a few hours. I didn't understand why the Lord would not see fit in His infinite wisdom to give His peace to me

---

[13]The guest house is a place the hospital offers at a minimal price, for families whose loved ones are in critical care in order to be close to them.

to "disperse the powers of darkness" from me (D&C 21:6). Yet, I would still continue to knock on heaven's door, waiting impatiently to be invited in.

As I lay down that night, my anxious mind and clamped heart kept sleep at bay. Like Enos in the Book of Mormon, "...my soul hungered; [so I knelt] down before my Maker, and I cried unto him in mighty prayer and supplication." I

> *"I am weary with my groaning: all the night make I my bed to swim; I water my couch with my tears." - Psalms 6:6*

had prayed all day, and now "when the night came I did still raise my voice high [hoping] that it reached the heavens" (Enos 1:4).

I wanted to lay my burden at the Lord's feet and for Him to take it away. I cried out to the Lord for deliverance, to escape the harrowing torment I was in. I explained to Him that there were many people praying for me to receive peace. And I reminded Him of others that had received peace - even when they had lost loved ones.

But I continued to battle the blackness, feeling that if I did not receive solace soon, my heart would break under the weight of my grief. This was the most ominous moment of my life, and I needed the darkness banished from my soul. The silence in the Heavens was deafening. Had not Christ said, "Come unto me, all ye that ...are heavy laden, and I will give you rest"? (Matthew 11:28). Why couldn't I receive this rest for my spirit? Why couldn't peace prevail? I lay awake the entire night and did "not cease to call upon God" (Moses 1:18), yet the pain continued even as I was persistent in my pleadings for healing.

As I continued to feel such intense agony of spirit, I became acquainted with God in a more intimate way. It was as if I had to go through my own minute Gethsemane to understand in a very limited way what the Savior endured for all of us. I gained a greater depth of appreciation for the Saviors words, "I have trodden this wine-press alone" (D&C 133:50). I know that He had been there with me all along, but I felt completely and utterly alone. The agony that threatened to wash over me and sink me in despair would not dissipate but seemed to stretch to eternity.

During the night I continued to remember Abraham. Knowing that it wasn't a coincidence that I had prepared to teach the lesson of Abraham and Isaac on the week of Lexi's accident should have made it much easier for me to believe that Lexi would be saved. Yet I found myself like the woman with the issue of blood, hiding timidly in a crowded market place wondering if someone as ordinary as myself could be worthy of asking for such a healing. Abraham was a prophet and I was… well, I was just like the woman with the issue of blood - not important enough to feel I should receive such a miracle.

However, as I thought of the story of the woman, I realized that by her actions, she was actually the only courageous person in the crowd. She believed with all her heart that if she could just touch the hem of the Savior's garment, she would be healed. She didn't even wait for Him to stop and acknowledge her or for Him to put His hands on her head to bless her. She just knew instinctively that His very being was so filled with power and glory that just by touching His clothing, she would be made whole. I wondered if I was putting a limit on His gift to us. Yet, I soon found out that as soon as I could touch the Savior and feel His love, I too was healed (Mark 5:25-34).

I hurried across the street to the hospital around 4:00 a.m. I had only slept a couple hours, so I thought I might as well go back. I had prayed all night, but I continued to pray into the morning by Lexi's bedside.

Soon, the whole room was bathed in the warm glow, as the early morning sunlight broke over the mountain and peeked through the windows. A warm sensation sent a wave of peace through my soul. It engulfed me, soothing my heart, the pain dissolving in its path. My aching wounds were replaced with joy and happiness as if the sun itself had chased away my darkness.

The light flooded into my heart, and a burst of warmth pressed into my breast. But it was not the sun, but *His Son* that brought this change. It was His peace that engulfed my soul. My heart was open to an understanding that a ram had been found: "the word of the

> *"It must needs be that this is a good seed, or that the word is good, for it beginneth to enlarge my soul; yea, it beginneth to enlighten my understanding, yea, it beginneth to be delicious to me." - Alma 32:28*

Lord came to me by the power of the Holy Ghost" (Moroni 8:7) with such clarity I knew that Lexi would be healed.

I felt to cry as Alma, "there could be nothing so exquisite and so bitter as were my pains …[and] on the other hand, there can be nothing so exquisite and sweet as was my joy" (Alma 36:21), Without warning, a single tear broke on my lap. Tilting my head back, I looked heavenward and whispered a reverent, "Thank you."

My voice quivered with emotion, pools of tears now clouding my vision. "I can't believe that you are letting her stay," I whispered in wonder and awe. The Spirit filled me. My emotions clawed at my throat; I didn't want to breathe. Tears streaked my cheeks but I didn't brush them away. Any movement I feared might allow the Spirit to flee. I wanted to capture this moment, to bask in its warmth. Could heaven be any closer than this?

A new-found power surged through me like an unquenchable fire burning in my breast. I stole a quick glance at Lexi. Then watching her intently, a twinge of excitement filled me, knowing that soon I'd see her smile, feel the kindness in her eyes, and hear her infectious laugh. I was overwhelmed with gratitude--I had not been forgotten. I dropped to my knees; a sob of joy tore from my soul.

When Jesus told his disciples that his friend Lazarus had died, He made an interesting statement: "And I am glad for your sakes that I was not there, to the intent ye may believe" (John 11:15). Was that the same lesson He was teaching me and which He teaches all of us when He allows us to suffer for a while so we might come to a greater understanding of belief, where belief turns into knowledge? The eternal gratitude I felt for Christ's suffering was now magnified fourfold. I had a personal reassurance that God was near, as He spoke to my heart, "I have heard thy prayer, I have seen thy tears: behold, I will heal thee" (2 Kings 20:5). The accompanying strength and courage received from the positive assurance that Lexi would be healed brought rejoicing, and my spirit soared.

Like the Psalmist, "I waited patiently for the Lord" to bring me comfort," and he inclined unto me, and heard my cry" (Psalm 40:1). What a miraculous healing for my spirit! I had received a witness "after the trial of [my] faith" (Ether 12:6). I was changed. I was no longer alone.

God truly does "succor his people according to their infirmities" (Alma 7:12). I had learned years earlier that succor means to "run to", which helped me visualize the Savior

> *When through the deep waters I call thee to go,*
> *The rivers of sorrow shall not thee o'erflow,*
> *For I will be with thee thy troubles to bless,*
> *And sanctify to thee thy deepest distress.*
>
> *The soul that on Jesus hath leaned for repose.*
> *I will not, I cannot, desert to his foes,*
> *That soul, though all hell should endeavor to shake,*
> *I'll never, no never, no never forsake.*
>
> *- "How Firm a Foundation," Included in the first LDS hymnbook, 1835. Pg. 6, Text: Attr. to Robert Keen, ca. 1787. Music: Attr. To J. Ellis, ca. 1889.*

running to my side in my hour of need, personalizing this scripture in a very tender way.

What a remarkable gift to *know,* even before she came out of her coma, that Lexi would stay with us and be whole and well again. I am grateful that the Lord loved me enough to stretch my soul and say in effect, "Call unto me, and I will answer thee, and shew thee great and mighty things, which thou knowest not" (Jeremiah 33:3).

CHAPTER NINE

THE MIRACLE OF CHARITY

"And we have known and believed the love that God hath to us. God is love; and he that dwelleth in love dwelleth in God, and God in him." - 1 John 4:16

If the ten-and-a-half-hour van ride didn't bond our family, the beach was sure to do it. A gentle sea breeze brushed through my hair as the kids scampered out of the van to the sun-drenched beach, sand squishing between their toes. With a family of eleven on a tight budget, going out to eat and plane  fares were out of the question. But the kids didn't seem to notice, as they bodysurfed through daring waves and flew kites on overcast days.

Plastic buckets swinging by their side, they collected seashells that had gently washed ashore as they soaked up the sun. They cheered when sand castles were left erect from

crushing waves and giggled when some became engulfed and washed mysteriously away as seagulls swooped overhead.

"If only our summers were endless," I mused. It was here that we found a place separating us from the rest of the world. It drew us back year after year. The kids were each other best friends and relished the time spent together. They were fiercely loyal to one another and learned to forgive easily when siblings disappointed. Many times people observing our

family commented on how impressed they were that they seemed to genuinely love and want to be with each other.

So it was a great joy when my children who lived out of state and their families finally began arriving Thursday morning, the day after Lexi's accident, to be together again. They had come with heavy and broken hearts, thinking they were returning to Utah to attend a funeral. Shelby and her husband, Brandon, arrived first with their boys; and then shortly after Cassidy and Daniel came with their son, Calvin.

My son JD and his wife, McCall, and his girls were last to arrive after a 15-hour flight delay. When I looked up to see JD walking towards me, we fought back tears as we hugged each other in a warm embrace. It had been a long day for both of us.

Although we were filled with sadness it was wonderful to be together again. We hugged, wept, and received strength from one another. Sharing together our pain seemed to lesson it. They gave me strength when I felt my soul was empty.

My children from out of state had been going through their own set of emotions. It was horrible for them to be so far away, without the support of the family. Lexi's sister

> *"I know in whom I have trusted... He hath filled me with his love, even unto the consuming of my flesh." -* 2 Nephi 4:19, 21

Cassidy told me how the night had seemed endless, filled with tears and more tears. She hated that she was not able to rush to the hospital that night, but had to wait until morning to leave, enduring a three-hour, grueling plane ride with no communication. It was torture. In flight she sobbed and prayed, and prayed and sobbed. At times she felt that Lexi would be all right, but doubts would soon sneak in, and she feared she would not make it.

Seventeen hours after Cassidy got the fateful call, she walked into Lexi's room. Her heart dropped. This was not Lexi. She was lifeless, very close to slipping away. She wanted so badly to have her wake up--to see her smile again. The thought that she might not ever talk to her again started to sneak into her mind and the tears returned with a vengeance. "Be strong for your family; they need you," she kept repeating to herself.

She walked to Lexi's side and touched her as if to wake her from this sleep. "Lexi it's me. Lexi don't leave. Lexi we need you," Cassidy pleaded. She felt like it was a dream. But despite all the terror she experienced up to that point, she felt a peace when she walked into her room, an immense power from on high.

Just ten years earlier I had struggled to say goodbye to my oldest son, McKay, who was going off to college just a mere thirty-minute drive away. Standing on our front porch, the entire family gathered and waved good-bye, tears welling up in our eyes. My heart knew our family would never be the same again. I tried to be strong and smother the thought, but I couldn't hold back the tears as my son pulled away from the house in his red beat up car, his belongings spilling from boxes piled high on the seats.

All of a sudden, he slammed on his brakes, pulled himself through the driver's side window, smiled broadly, and, while pounding his fist in the air, shouted, "Hurrah for Israel! Hurrah for Israel! Hurrah for Israel!"

Instantly the mood changed. Tears soon forgotten as cheers erupted, "Hurrah for Israel, Hurrah for Israel!"

we shouted back, grinning wildly. The exuberance was catching, and as his car drove off, we sprinted from the porch, chasing him down the street cheering wildly and as loudly as we could, hoping that he would hear us as we continued to chant, "Hurrah, hurrah for Israel." The splatter of bare feet against the pavement persisted until he turned a corner and the car was a distant memory.

A family night[14] lesson had sparked McKay's actions. Years earlier I had told them the story about Brigham Young and Heber C. Kimball who had been called to serve as missionaries in Great Britain. The day they were

---

[14]Our church encourages families to get together every Monday night to teach about the Savior and the principals He espoused. It's also a night to create a special bond between siblings and where games are played.

to leave, they both were deathly ill, along with their families.

Heber told of the experience, "It was with difficulty we got into the wagon, I thought my very inmost parts would melt leaving my family, almost in the arms of death. I said to Brother Brigham, 'Let's rise up and give them a cheer.' We arose, and swinging our hats three times over our heads, shouted: 'Hurrah, hurrah for Israel.' Vilate (Heber's wife) arose from her bed. She had a smile on her face. Vilate and Mary Anne Young (Brigham's Wife) cried out to us. 'Goodbye, God bless you.'"(LDS.org Church History in the Fullness of Times Student Manual. Chapter 18. The Mission of the Twelve. (2003) 225-239.)

McKay knew instinctively that this cheer would do the same for our family. But it did more than boost our spirits; there was an unspoken message that no matter what happened to us when we were apart, we would remain faithful and true to God, even during the hard times. If it had been appropriate in the hospital that cheer would have erupted again. We would be steadfast, even if we were to lose our Lexi--our daughter, our sister, our friend.

As we gathered in Lexi's room one of the first things we each

"But the fruit of the spirit is love." - Gal. 5:22

thought about was what our last communication had been with

her. While we were discussing our last interaction, we found that all of us had made contact with her sometime in the last week and that everyone had ended their conversation by saying to Lexi that they loved her. We felt a sense of relief as we realized that we had prioritized staying in contact with each other, that there was no tinge of regret.

The kids don't always communicate with each other weekly, but it was a tender mercy from God that He had prompted each of them to contact Lexi in some way that week. It seemed to lift our individual burden just a little, knowing that we had just recently reached out to her and expressed to her our love. An even greater feeling came as we reflected on our conversations and realized that not one person had said an unkind word to her in recent memory. There were no regrets and no feelings of guilt. I realized I wouldn't have even been able to breathe if there had even been a sharp tone in my recent words to Lexi. Our family is not perfect, but in this instance we were grateful to be able to see that we had done things right.

Lexi made it easy for the family to express their love openly because whenever any of her siblings left our house after coming over for dinner or for a visit, Lexi would rush to the door, give them a hug, and tell them that she loved them. Those individuals that had just married into the family were surprised by her spontaneous and

> *"Above all these things put on charity."* - Col. 3:14

childlike expression. But as soon as they joined the family, there was never a visit that she didn't utter the words "I love you" to them as well.

It is a goal of ours, like I'm sure it is with almost every family, to not let disputes, contentious feelings or disagreements carry on day after day. As the scriptures teach, "Let there be no strife, I pray thee, between me and thee… for we be brethren," (Genesis 13:8).

When my children were young, instead of sending them to their rooms for time-out when they said or did something unkind to their siblings, I had them go to their rooms and write a note about something good they saw in the sibling they had quarreled with. It was gratifying to see how quickly their hearts would change and a feeling of love reenter our home by that simple act to "strengthen [each other] in all [our] conversation, in all [our] prayers, and in all [our] doings," (D&C 108:7).

The days continued to pass slowly as we waited for Lexi to come out of her coma, but now we were together, and that made all the difference. Each day we would kneel together in family prayer, thanking God for the small miracles we would see throughout the day. When we were blessed to have our entire family allowed in Lexi's room, we experienced a tiny slice of heaven as we knelt down in a circle around her bed holding hands The spirit was always so intense that we felt like what we were getting a small glimpse of what Zion would be like as we continued to bear one another's burdens. A familiar feeling of heaven no longer seemed out of reach. I didn't want the warmth and the unique strength that these quiet, sacred moments to dissolve.

I had been blessed to be "born of goodly parents" (1 Nephi1:1). The principles my parents espoused shaped my life. They were rooted deeply in my soul from a young age. Those were joyful days with my parents, and the memories came easily as I sat next to Lexi pondering.

It was dark outside when suddenly I was awakened to music blasting through the house. Within minutes of being disturbed at such an unearthly hour, my door swung open wide, and the light turned on. Squinting and trying to adjust my eyes to the brightness, I saw my dad standing in the doorway smiling broadly as he sang, "Top of the morning, it's a bright and sunny day, eggs over easy just to chase your cares away."

How I wanted to sink back down into my cozy pillow and get a few more winks before I had to go to school, but the music was too loud. Besides that, I could hear my mom bustling around in the kitchen getting breakfast ready, so it would be futile to try to go back to sleep. If it weren't for the smell of waffles and bacon and the cheeriness of my dad's voice, it would have been a challenge to get up in the wee morning hours for our regular family scripture study, before the sun dared show its face.

My parents knew that without anchoring our souls in God, we would be unprepared for the Lord's coming, like the foolish virgins who "slumbered and slept" while the bridegroom tarried (Matt. 25:5). It was these early mornings and the Monday nights where we prayed, sang, and learned about the Savior together that rooted my mind and heart so deeply to God and taught me that He would not forsake me. Those times shaped my life.

The scriptures were an anchor to me in the storm that

> *"Call unto me, and I will answer thee, and shew thee great and mighty things, which thou knowest not." - Jeremiah 33:3*

came barreling through my world when Lexi was given less than a 1% chance of survival. They were the reason I was not carried away in the whirlwind of lost hope and despair. Yoking myself to God before the storm hit was paramount. And as long as I remembered to "stand…still," and to "fear not, nor be dismayed," but "to believe in the Lord," I knew that the "Lord [would] be with [me]" (2 Chronicles 20:17, 20).

It was my parent's example that helped me to be like Nehemiah in the Old Testament who said, "I am doing a great work, so that I cannot come down: why should the work cease, whilst I leave it, and come down to you?" (Nehemiah 6:1-4). I wanted to raise my children with that same level of commitment, where nothing--sports, activities, or friends--

would come before God's teachings. Every single Monday night and every single morning would be devoted to learning from the scriptures and trying to become more like God. No exceptions. I have come to know and see that the scriptures were and continue to be a protective shield from the threatening war of the world surrounding the hearts of my family. Now as we sat in the same room, I looked lovingly at each person, my heart full to overflowing, thinking of their integrity and righteousness.

Even though our family has always been close, I could tell that being here with Lexi was drawing us together in a deeper bond as we literally clung to one another, both body and spirit. We began to notice we were developing more love for each other.

I remember one afternoon sitting with my daughter-in-law McCall by Lexi's bed. Neither of us talking--because we needed her room quiet in order for her brain to heal--but both of us understanding each other's pain. As I sat in that spiritual place, I felt my love growing stronger, not only for Lexi, but also for McCall. This love increased the same way with each member of my family as we spent hour after hour in Lexi's room. How blessed we were to have a greater outpouring of love come into our hearts for each other. This was as a "holy temple" to us (Jonah 2:7).

My daughter Cassidy explains our feelings perfectly:

"The thing I will always remember about this whole experience is the immense love that embraced my family. The moment I arrived at the hospital I felt love, a pure love, for each one of my family members. As we gathered for many family prayers, I felt love. I felt love as we sat quietly in Lexi's room. For the next few days, it was as if time stood still and nothing else in the world mattered--and

nothing did, except for my family and my knowledge of the gospel. The love we had for each other was magnified deeply, and it continued to grow with each passing day. There was no quarrel or disputations among us, but only love, kindness, gratitude, and selflessness towards one another. For me, it felt as if we were living in a piece of heaven. We were all striving for goodness, so our Lexi would be healed."

The bond of love and the faith we shared strengthened us and carried us through this very difficult time. Through our faith we were able to cast our fears aside and strive for a perfect love. Just as John declared, "There is no fear in love; but perfect love casteth out fear" (1 John 4:18). Although we may not always understand the Lord's purpose, recognizing

His deep love for us assures us that we can always trust in Him.

As Nancy Murphy, a professor of Christian philosophy, explains in her book *Whisperings of the Spirit*, "During the difficult times of our lives, we can imagine the Lord asking, 'Do you know why this is happening to you?' With complete faith in his infinite wisdom and his eternal perspective, we can then say to him, 'No, but you do" (pg 51).

Cassidy continues:

"The Lord knows all things and in His wisdom, He knows what will bring about the most rapid spiritual growth in our lives, moving us as quickly as possible along the path to perfection. This accelerated spiritual progression many times comes as a result of our trials. Despite difficulty and pain, it is in this way that challenges can greatly bless our lives.

Our family has been a witness of his, and I know as we strive to love and trust in the Lord we will be able to endure all things. When we cast away our fears and love perfectly, all things will become brighter and we will see how the Lord sees us and our fellow men. May we all strive to embrace each other with a perfect love."

The perfect love Cassidy describes is called charity in the scriptures: "Charity suffereth long, and is kind; charity envieth not; charity vaunteth not itself, is not puffed up Doth not behave itself unseemingly, seeketh not her own, is not easily provoked, thinketh no evil; Rejoiceth not in iniquity, but rejoiceth in the truth; Beareth all things, believeth all things, hopeth all things, endureth all things…And now abideth faith, hope, charity, these three; but the greatest of these is charity" (1 Corinthians 13: 4-7, 13).

CHAPTER TEN

THE MIRACLE TO KNOW THE
HEAVENS ARE NOT SILENT

"Wherefore, my beloved brethren, have miracles ceased because Christ hath ascended into heaven, and hath sat down on the right hand of God...? Behold I say unto you, Nay;" - Moroni 7: 27, 29

My son, Parker, is only a year younger than Lexi. It was hard for both of them to be at the tail end of the family because  it seemed like overnight their five siblings who had been living at home went off to college or got married (two had left two years before).It was just the two of them at home when Lexi started high school - a family of nine children down to two in a few years. Being at the end of our big family, they have always been close, and they have always considered each other best friends.

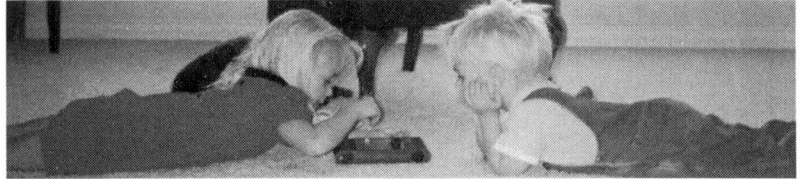

Lexi was the perfect older sister, watching out for Parker's every need. If his friends were busy on a Saturday night, she had him tag along with her - even if she had a date.

He was the one she would confide in about boys, and he in turn divulged to her his secret crushes. He was her sidekick--the one she would call upon to go with her on her spontaneous adventurous.

On one of their favorite outings they rounded a bend along the river bank ducking to miss the low overhanging branches that lined the river enclosing their secluded hideout. The forest of trees wrapped around the edge of the bank making it almost impossible to discover, forming a canopy of sorts to hide their secret. It was Lexi's favorite place to go. It beckoned to her of freedom. And the cluster of trees provided needed shade on a warm, muggy day.

As they entered the clearing, Lexi could hardly contain her excitement. Pushing off with her right foot, she launched from the bridge, gliding effortlessly through the air and then striking the water. Her eyes showed no fear. Floating in the river, she drifted a few yards, fending off some low-level branches until she found a large, sturdy branch with which to pull herself out to the far bank.

The current was not strong enough to sweep her farther down, but the icy cold water forced her to retreat. A few feeble rays of sun slipped through the trees, pouring much-needed heat through her entire body. She felt freer than a bird suddenly released from its cage.

Parker followed suit, sailing through the air, knees tucked tight under his chin, hitting the water with a mighty

splash. He waded out up onto the rocks, drops of water lingering on his skin, as he playfully shook his dripping hair, spraying Lexi.

Goosebumps spread over her arms and legs as the wind rustled through the aspens. She pulled her knees close to her chest and wrapped her arms snugly around them, having forgotten their towels. This was the life. Parker knew his world could never be dull when Lexi was with him. The twinkle in her eyes was forever present.

Now, the possibility of them being separated forever during this earth life was too much for him to handle. For the first few nights in the hospital, Parker was beyond devastated at the thought of losing his sister, his best friend. He thought many times, "I can't lose Lexi! I don't know what I'd do without her. You can't do this to me Heavenly Father!"

After two days of turmoil, he was desperate for peace and willing to accept whatever the Lord had in store for his sister. He went home from the hospital that evening and prayed to Heavenly Father asking for peace. After he prayed, he felt inspired to open up his scriptures. As he did, they fell open to Mormon 9:11-19, and these are the words he read:

"But behold, I will show unto you a God of miracles…And now, O all ye that have imagined up unto yourselves a god who can do no miracles, I would ask of you, have all these things passed of which I have spoken?…Behold I say unto you, Nay; and God has not ceased to be a God of miracles… And who shall say that Jesus Christ did not do many mighty miracles? And there were many mighty miracles wrought by the hands of the apostles. And if there were miracles wrought then, why has God ceased to be a God of miracles and yet be an unchangeable Being? And behold, I say unto you he changeth not; if so he would cease to be God; and he ceaseth not to be God, and is a God of miracles. Behold I

say unto you that whoso believeth in Christ, doubting nothing...it shall be granted unto him" (Mormon 9: 11, 15, 18-19, 21, emphasis added).

As Parker read these verses, written long ago by an ancient prophet, he felt an overpowering sense of comfort and knew that Lexi would be alright. He had read these words before but had just skimmed them, not really understanding what they meant, as he had not been a witness to any miracles in our day. But now these same words pierced his heart and spoke comfort to him. He knew they were true! Of course God was still a God of miracles. He loves all His children the same whether they were born in this century or during Christ's lifetime.

Tears welled up in his eyes - his mourning changed to joy for the first time since the accident. He knew this was a direct answer from the Lord because of the fervent prayers he had offered on Lexi's behalf. In the scriptures, he had found comfort from The Prince of Peace. He knelt down and thanked Heavenly Father for showing him those exact verses. Hope was now his companion as his soul expanded with faith.

Early the next morning, Parker couldn't wait to return to the hospital. With an air of calm, he hurried to the ICU where he found me seated, as usual, beside Lexi's bed and pulled up a chair. He had his scriptures with him and opened to the exact spot he had read the night before. His voice trembled slightly with emotion as he whispered, "Mom, I know Lexi will be ok."

I looked at him quizzically, waiting for him to finish. He pushed the scriptures toward me, his voice lowered even more and began to tell me of his experience the night before.

> *"For neither at any time hath any wrought miracles until after their faith; wherefore they first believed in the Son of God." - Ether 12:18*

After I read the passage for myself, we both looked at each and smiled as tears trickled down our faces. I was astonished at how explicit his answer was, leaving no room for confusion or doubt. What a testimony to Parker that God knew him and knew of his love for his sister that He chose to send a direct message to him that Lexi would live.

Parker's faith and diligence in listening to the Spirit was another witness for me and my family that Lexi would be made whole. As we pondered this gift our Heavenly Father had given to him, our faith was unshaken in the knowledge that God's hand was in every detail of this miracle. It was true that if we put our "trust in God," we would "be supported in [our] trials, and [our] troubles..." (Alma 36:3). We knew for ourselves that it was God who would make Lexi whole again. It was amazing

"Blessed is the man that trusteth in the Lord, and whose hope the Lord is." - Jeremiah 17:7

to see how Parker's demeanor had changed. He was happy again. There was no room for fear. He *knew* nothing doubting.

I needed these constant reminders from my family that it *was* God's will that Lexi be made whole. Because the prognosis given by each doctor was grim, we knew her healing would be nothing short of a miracle. Parker's words continued to keep me in a good place, especially as Lexi continued to struggle. That passage of scripture would forever burn within.

Shortly after this, my son JD joined us in the room and remarked, "Even lying on this hospital bed in a coma, she is stunning." The other family members in the room agreed, nodding thoughtfully. One of them said, "That's just what I have been thinking."

I glanced over at Lexi, and I too was astonished at her uncommon beauty. She was pretty but unpretentious. No one would have ever guessed by looking at her that she was a hard worker who toiled in the soil. At 5'7", she had a slim frame and flawless olive skin, which deepened due to endless hours of tennis and outside labor. But her arms and hands were still smooth and delicate.

I had always been amazed at her work ethic. A typical Saturday morning in our house meant that there would

"The ancient evil of greed shows its face in the assertion of entitlement: I am entitled to this or that because of who I am—a son or a daughter, a citizen, a victim, or a member of some other group. Entitlement is generally selfish. It demands much, and it gives little or nothing." - Elder Dallin H. Oaks, "Unselfish Service," Ensign, May 2009.

be no sleeping in, even though all my kids were teenagers now. I would hear footsteps below my room at about 6:30 am, the kids in the kitchen getting their breakfast before hitching up the trailer with the lawn mower to take off for their landscaping business.

Saturday was Lexi's busiest day. She mowed, edged, and weeded until 11 a.m., then got a quick bite before taking off to practice tennis. After tennis, she would have a few hours to study before changing her clothes to waitress at a nearby restaurant. She worked tirelessly for her money and saved almost every penny to pay for college and for her mission. She was shocked to hear a friend tell her that she didn't need to work because she would just have the government pay for her schooling and needs. That attitude was prevalent among many in her age group and made her frustrated and sad. Instead of choosing that same easy route she pushed on with determination.

Returning to our conversation in Lexi's hospital room, I said, "You know, there are two things I miss most about Lexi. One is seeing her blue eyes. They are so full of life."

Then turning to look at my son JD, I questioned, "Didn't you feel that through her eyes you could see her trusting heart?" He nodded in agreement.

Then, cocking my head to my left to look at Parker, I continued, "And what do you think is the second attribute that I have yearned to see again? In unison both my boys said confidently, "Her smile."

"Yup. It was electrifying," I said. It was easy to see they concurred with my assessment.

"And now all of us know for ourselves that the heavens aren't silent. It's just a matter of time until we see her smile again. God has spoken to each of us and His words couldn't have been clearer than those he spoke to Parker when he directed him to that passage of scripture in Moroni. God has been so good and kind to our family. As our prophet, President Monsen has said, 'The Lord is in the details of our lives.'"

My daughter Shelby explains:

"The most profound lesson I learned through this was how important personal revelation is. I was reminded that the Lord answers prayer. I learned the importance of trusting the Lord. Before Lexi's accident, I always prayed but didn't have the faith that I do now that He would help me. Now I can't go a day without asking for guidance, or help for a specific challenge. It's crazy that I never used this power to the extent that I could have. We all have trials. Some come in the form of finances, marriage or children or in ways we don't usually think about like feelings of loneliness, unfulfilled hopes and dreams. Moreover, with every challenge the Lord pleads that we will come to Him in prayer. The Lord is there; He will give us personal revelation and answer our prayers. Whether your challenges or questions are big or small, He cares."

CHAPTER ELEVEN

THE MIRACLE OF STANDING FIRMLY IN FAITH

"And he said, The Lord is my rock, and my fortress, and my deliverer; The God of my rock; in him will I trust: he is my shield, and the horn of my salvation, my high tower, and my refuge, my saviour; thou savest me from violence." - 2 Samuel 22:2-3

I had been given the knowledge through the Holy Ghost that Lexi would be healed and go on to live a normal life. This assurance came through private and family prayers, coupled with priesthood blessings and personal revelation.

All of the priesthood blessings that Lexi received were powerful and direct, testifying that she would be healed. Yet it was easy to fall from that level of faith whenever a doctor or therapist came to check on her, as they would always repeat the same prognosis that Lexi's chances of making it were slim. They would remind me that for the next five to seven days the probability of losing Lexi was still very high, and that even if she did survive, she'd most likely end up in a care center for the rest of her life because of the shearing that had occurred in her brain.

As they were the experts, I'd allow doubts to creep back into my mind and create a distance from God's promise to me. Their words forced a battle to rage between my mind and my heart which would chip away at my faith and my hope would flee. Yet I knew that God "workest *after* men have faith" (Ether 12:30, emphasis added). I couldn't allow the doctors bleak, but honest, evaluations stop me from having the faith of Jared who could even move mountains.

It wasn't hard to realize while I pondered these scriptures that faith was paramount to her healing. In fact I'd been taught that faith *is* equal to power. (Joseph Smith)

Just as the people thronged Jesus, I felt myself pushing with all my might through an invisible crowd to be near Him, to feel of His love and of His comfort and to keep my faith strong (see Luke 8:42).

There was one therapist who I remember particularly for his cheerful countenance. He was positive and happy and told me not to worry. He had seen many patients who had been hit by cars recover, as long as they hit the windshield and not

the metal bar above the windshield. For those people who do hit the bar, there is no hope because the bar does not give.

I flinched at his words and my faith faltered. Interrupting, I told him that is exactly where Lexi's head had hit the car. His countenance changed abruptly, and an uncomfortable silence filled the air.

> *And it was "By faith Enoch was translated that he should not see death" It was "By faith Noah being warned of God of things not seen as yet...prepared an ark to the saving of his house." Again it was "By faith Moses...passed through the Red sea as by dry land: which the Egyptians assaying to do were drowned." And finally, it was "By faith the walls of Jericho fell down, after they were compassed about seven days."*
> *- Hebrews 11:5,7,23,29,30.*

His eyes dropped to look down at his feet, and refusing to look me in the eye, he manage to mutter, "I'm sorry," before looking away. Again my faith dipped a little."

The outlook was never positive from a medical stand point but we had been promised in priesthood blessings that she would be fully healed both body and spirit. Additionally I had been given my own personal witness. I knew and had faith in those promises, but I still couldn't help occasionally slipping into a feeling of hopelessness when every professional said otherwise and when I saw all the pieces of evidence around me. I had only needed to look to the book of Hebrews for my direction. "Cast not away therefore (your) confidence, which hath great recompense of reward. For ye have need of patience, that after ye have done the will of God, ye might receive the promise." (Hebrews 10:35-36)

It was only *after* David had faith that he could go face the giant Goliath. I too had to have this faith *before* the miracle could happen. I needed to keep these scripture stories foremost in my mind. Faith was the key. Yet sometimes I felt the weight of my fear becoming so heavy, I could not feel the lightness the Spirit brings. Why couldn't I be as Enoch, whose faith was so great that "he spake the word of the Lord, and the earth trembled and the mountains fled"? (Moses 7:13). My courage could not falter. I could "not be afraid of their faces…:" (Jeremiah 1:8) for it was God that said "..I have made thee this day a defenced city, and an iron pillar and …against the people of the land. And they shall fight against thee; but they shall not prevail against thee; for I am with thee;..to deliver thee." (Jeremiah 1:18-19)

On the afternoon of the second day after the accident, I realized what my problem was. In the New Testament, there is a beautiful passage describing how the Savior walks on the sea to his disciples who are in a ship. When Peter asks the Savior if he can walk out to Him, the Lord invites him to come. And when Peter's eyes are focused on the Savior, he is able to walk on the water, but when he looks away from Him, the waves become daunting, and he sinks.

I had kept my eyes focused on the Savior, but, like Peter, when I saw the rough waves and strong, boisterous winds come, I stopped looking towards Christ and would begin to sink. I felt to cry out as did Peter, "Lord save me" (Matthew 14:30). Could I rid myself of this fear and continue to be fixed on Heaven's purpose and reach up to grasp the Savior's outstretched hand? For I knew that "God hath not given us the spirit of fear; but of power, and of love, and of a sound mind" (2 Timothy 1:7).

"Be still, my soul: Thy God doth undertake, To guide the future as he has the past. Thy hope, thy confidence let nothing shake. All now mysterious shall be bright at last. Be still, my soul: The waves and winds still know His voice who ruled them while he dwelt below." - "Be Still, My Soul," Hymns, no.124 Text: Katharina von Schlegel, b. 1697;trans. by Jane Borthwick, 1813-1897

Fear was my stumbling block. I needed to be reminded of the Lord's limitless power and to turn to Him with full purpose of heart, "for with God nothing [is] impossible" (Luke 1:37). I decided I needed to have a visual image of the Savior in my mind the next time a doctor came into the room.

A few minutes after making this plan, the Lord tested me. A doctor came in to explain, yet again, what the outcome for Lexi was probably going to be. I began the challenge of fastening my eyes only on the Savior.

111

Although the doctor thought I was looking at him, my eyes were instead fixed on an image in my mind of the Savior next to him, and I could feel the Savior's gaze upon me and hear His words telling me to "be of good cheer" (Acts 23:11). As I saw Christ in my mind's eye, my soul was immediately filled with the fire of faith. When the doctor was finished talking, I realized my faith was still intact. I had pushed back against my weakness that had threatened my resolve, and I had not let their words wash over me and sink me into despair. Shortly after the doctor left my daughter Cassidy came into the room and I excitedly told her, "I didn't sink! I didn't sink!" I hugged her and she rejoiced with me in my feat. I had asked, believing that I'd receive, and it was given unto me (3 Nephi 18:20).

I had learned an important lesson of choosing faith and hope instead of fear. From that point on, this is how I made it through each of the doctors' visits. I was "filled" with the spirit of hope (3 Nephi 18:4). For me the doctor's words were as daunting as the storm Peter faced, but our Savior has said, "...therefore walk with me," (Moses 6:34) and that is what I learned to do.

Do we accept God's offer to walk with him by standing firmly in faith? In Acts 16: 23 it says Paul and Silas "had many stripes laid upon them, [and the rulers] cast them into prison." Their life seemed bleak indeed. Yet, in verse 25 it says, "And at midnight Paul and Silas prayed, and sang praises unto God." They chose to walk with God in faith, joy, and thanksgiving.

I also learned through this experience that when I did sink, the Savior's hand was outstretched ready to lift me back up to His side, just as he did for Peter: "And *immediately* Jesus stretched forth his hand, and caught him" (Matt 14:31).

The hand of Christ had already come to me in many different ways. It

> *"...his hand is outstretched still." - Isaiah 9:12).*

came to me when my son Tanner bore his testimony to me, when my son Parker told me of his sacred experience that God was still a God of miracles, and when my son, JD shared a

several scripture stories with me. I realized that each time I had struggled to maintain that level of faith that was needed for a miracle, His hand was always there through someone else, waiting for me to reach out, grasp it, and hold on.

Each of them had learned from Christ's example how to extend an outstretched hand. Just as Pater, having learned the power that came from Christ's outstretched hand when he began to sink, was able to extend this same gift to others after Christ's resurrection. In Joppa, a woman named Tabitha died; and Peter" gave her his hand, and lifted her up." (Acts 941).

Another scripture story that took on new meaning after Lexi's accident is the story of Gideon in the Old Testament. The children of Israel were in bondage to the Midianites when an angel of the Lord appeared unto Gideon and told him the Lord was with him. Gideon said, "Oh my Lord, if the Lord be with us, why then is all this befallen us? and where be all his miracles which our fathers told us of saying, Did not the Lord bring us up from Egypt? but now the Lord hath forsaken us and delivered us into the hands of the Midianites" (Judges 6:13)

"Yes," I thought, "Why has this befallen us? Where are the miracles that happened before?" And just as Gideon needed to have several signs, or assurances, from God before having the faith to go to battle, I realized I needed those same assurances.

The scriptures continue, "And the Lord looked upon him and said, Go in this thy might, and thou shalt save Israel from the hand of the Midianites: have not I sent thee?"(Judges 6:14). Our family, through priesthood blessings, was given a similar promise--that Lexi would be saved from death and make a full recovery. These priesthood blessings brought comfort, yet part of me was like Gideon, as he replied to the Lord, "Oh my Lord, wherewith shall I save Israel? behold, my family is poor in Manasseh, and I am the least in my father's house" (Judges 6:15).

I, too, wondered why the Lord would choose our family to perform this great miracle when so many other families have lost loved ones to untimely deaths. Our family would be considered the least in the world's view. We were not rich or powerful or famous. Could miracles happen in our day just as when Christ healed the sick, made the lame to walk, and the blind to see?

Even though Gideon was told, "The Lord is with thee," (Judges 6:12) he was understandably wary that the Lord would indeed perform a miracle for his people as He had done for Moses. Would God use him to help defeat such a fearsome foe as the Midianites? Gideon wanted unshakable faith, greater courage to leave his skepticism behind, so he asked for a sign. He told the Lord, "Behold, I will put a fleece of wool in the floor; and if the dew be on the fleece only, and it be dry upon all the earth beside then shall I know that thou wilt save Israel....And it was so" (Judges 6:37-38).

Needing that reassurance myself, I found my "signs" in the scriptures. I gained courage and my faith grew when I read about Gideon, Elisha, Joshua, and other prophets. Elisha reminded his servant to not be afraid because, "they that be

with us are more than they that be with them" (2Kings 6:16).
And Joshua taught his people to "be strong and of a good
courage" (Joshua 1:6).

Standing "...firm in
the faith of Christ.: -
Alma 48:13.

After Gideon received signs
from the Lord, he faithfully reduced
his army from 32,000 to 300 men so
that "Israel [might not] vaunt themselves against [the Lord]
saying, Mine own hand hath saved me" (Judges 7:2). As I
prepared to go to battle against a vast army of doctors, nurses,
and therapists reinforced with their knowledge and expertise
that Lexi's brain injury was too insurmountable to overcome, I
felt a lot like Gideon. I have never been more grateful for these
words spoken to Gideon and to all of us: "The Lord is with
thee" (Judges 6: 12). Now I could go forward and say, Yes, a
GCS[15] score of 3 can still win when the Lord is in charge of the
healing."

If Lexi's injuries had consisted of broken bones,
fractured ribs, or even a concussion--but had not been life-
threatening--people might have focused their attention solely
on Lexi and left God out of the picture. For instance, they
might have said that she was healed because she was a fighter
and could overcome anything. Yet, because her injuries were

---

[15]A GCS (Glasgow Coma Scale) score is used to evaluate
how conscious and responsive someone is after a traumatic brain
injury and to help gauge the severity of the injury. A 3 is the lowest
possible score.

so severe and the doctors gave her less than 1% chance to live, the focus when she did recover was really not on Lexi and her ability to fight to survive. It was on God and His goodness and might.

This focus on God's power was where it should have been and should always be. Our family talks about this miracle using the words, "God is amazing," or, "God is a God of miracles." If someone tries to give the credit to Lexi or to the doctors, I immediately correct them and let them know that although Lexi is a fighter and a good girl and the doctors were extremely capable and did a lot to help her, in the end it was God who saw fit in His infinite wisdom to extend her life for a season. We stand firmly in our faith with that conviction.

CHAPTER TWELVE

THE MIRACLE OF LOOKING UP

"Or have angels ceased to appear unto the children of men?...Behold I say unto you, Nay; for...it is by faith that angels appear and minister unto men." - Moroni 7:36-37

On February 28th, two days after the accident, the doctor came in and tried to wake up Lexi. He called out her name loudly, over and over, to get her to open her eyes. When she didn't respond, he gave her a hard pinch under the armpit which caused her to grimace in pain, and her eyes blinked open for a split second. Although I didn't like watching her experience pain, I was relieved to see her eyes open, even if only for a minute.

He then started tapping her thumb and asked her to give him a thumbs up with her left hand. She opened her eyes again, and there seemed to be a slight movement in her thumb, but then her eyes closed, and she lay still. He repeated this same thing on her right side, but this time, there was no reaction. After seeing no response, he continued to pinch her harder and harder and speak to her louder and louder. After doing this several times, she finally raised the left thumb just enough so that it was obvious to all of us she understood the command.

We squealed with excitement! Just seeing this slight movement in her thumb gave us hope. It was an important milestone on her long road to recovery, but also a foreshadowing of the trials to come in her efforts to gain her abilities back. The good news spread through the hospital as, later that day, I saw the attendant who helped us the night Lexi was brought in. Before I could say a word, he gave me a thumbs up, showing he had already heard the great news. We both were beaming!

The ICU had a rule that only two visitors were allowed into a patient's room at a time, so the members of our family had to trade off time with Lexi. 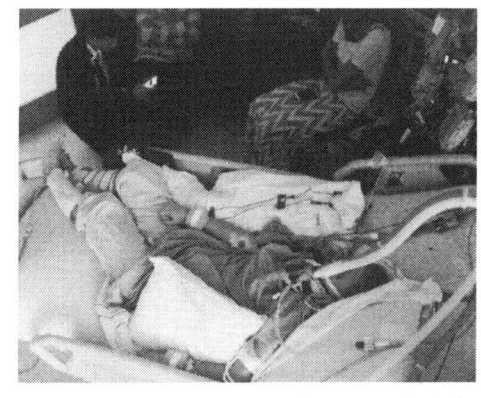 Luckily, I wasn't counted as part of that number and was allowed to stay in her room and take care of her instead of only being permitted to come in occasionally like the rest of the family.

As I spent more time in her room, I began to feel

> *"...you can have sacred, revelatory, profoundly instructive experience with the Lord in the most miserable experiences of your life—in the worst settings, while enduring the most painful injustices, when facing the most insurmountable odds and opposition you have ever faced." - Jeffrey R. Holland, "Lessons from Liberty Jail," CES Devotional, September*

disconnected from the world and could "stop and stand still" (D&C 5:34). Often my children tried to get me to go out into the waiting room to talk with the various visitors who came to the hospital to give us support and comfort. They assumed it would be good for me to get my mind off of Lexi by stepping away from the constant interruptions of therapists, nurses, and doctor--if only for a few minutes. But I couldn't leave for two reasons: First, I wanted to be right by Lexi's side at all times, and, second, I could feel beings on the other side of the veil[16] strengthening me.

On Saturday morning, I sat communing with God, unaware of the doctors and nurses coming in and out of Lexi's room or the beeping sound of machines monitoring her every movement. It felt good to finally have that transformation of peace seep deep into my soul. I could see the hand of God and

---

[16] It is a veil, not a wall that separates us from the spirit world. Veils can become thin, even parted. They who have preceded us in this work are very close to us. and minister here, (Boyd K Packer)

"We are often so busy and the world is so loud that it is difficult to hear the heavenly words "be still and know that I am God." - M. Russell Ballard, "Be Still, and Know That I am God," CES Devotional, May 2014

His grace manifested in my life more clearly as I reflected on all the events that had transpired in the days previous. The day before, I had felt trapped in a tunnel of darkness, grief, and uncertainty as I plead to understand God's will - a stark contrast from the solace I now felt as I became enveloped in God's love.

Perhaps from an outsider's view, Lexi's hospital room would have looked sterile, dreary, and even depressing. Yet it had become a temple for me.[17] My children who took turns rotating in throughout each day thought of it as a temple as well, bringing their scriptures to study, ponder, and pray in that holy setting. My son JD had been reading a few talks from one of our church's apostles, and he was eager to share with me the messages he felt would be important for me to hear. While the minutes and hours of the past few days had slugged by, the time was now bathed in light. I was grateful that my devotion to the scriptures had been cemented early in my life, as God's written word now echoed in my heart.

---

[17]See Jeffrey R. Holland, "Lessons from Liberty Jail," CES Devotional, September 2009.

But after a couple of sleepless nights sitting by the hospital bed holding Lexi's hand, my children insisted that I drive back to our house at night to get some sleep. They promised me that they would each take shifts during the night, knowing I would not leave Lexi's side unless I knew someone would be there with her. Even though my children and their spouses were exhausted, they were still willing to sacrifice their sleep for Lexi. I was grateful for my children's offer and was impressed with the love that they showed for their little sister. But I still felt a twinge of remorse leaving her side. I would not have been able to leave had they not stayed.

However, leaving Lexi's room full of angelic visitors ended up being very hard for me to do. There was great power when the seen and unseen worlds met. A familiar feeling swept through the space and pressed into my heart the first night I stayed with her, and it stretched on through the comings weeks. I knew there were many from the other side[18] who had come to be with Lexi, lifting some of the sorrow and bleakness from my heart. While in her room I felt elevated spiritually by the divine help given me, primarily from my parents who had passed on. It brought a power that seemed tangible. I whispered into

---

[18] We believe that after we die we pass on to the 'other side' which is near us here on earth so they can watch out for our welfare and help us. "We live in their presence, they see us, they are solicitous for our welfare, they love us now more than ever." (Elder Richard G. Scott)

the silence of the room the first night, choking out the words that I needed their help, in particular for my dad to give Lexi a blessing. I *knew* they were there. I was blessed to linger in their presence hour after hour, to feel the calmness of the gentle spirit they brought. I learned how very thin the veil is between us and our loved ones who have passed on. And I could feel a change coming over me

> *"If you live up to your privileges, the angels cannot be restrained from being your associates.""* - *Joseph Smith, History of the Church, 4:604-5. Apr. 28, 1842, reported by Eliza R. Snow.*

A week later, Lexi confirmed what I felt and knew. My daughter Cassidy and I asked Lexi if she remembered anything during the time when she was in the coma, particularly if someone she knew who had passed on had come to help her. She told us that Grandma and Grandpa were there (my parents) and that little children were there. About a week after, we asked her for more details about who and what she had seen. This second time, however, she informed us that sadly she had forgotten everything from when she was in the coma. Her memory of those events was gone. In fact Lexi had no recollection of even telling us earlier about seeing angelic visitors and was thrilled to know that her sister Cassidy had thought to record her words. Although Lexi confirmed what I felt, it didn't make my knowledge of what had happened any more sure. On the contrary, my experience with those visiting loved ones was a much more powerful witness for me; I knew they were there, and I didn't need anyone to tell me.

This is another example of how the stories I had read in the scriptures seemed to be

> *"Be not forgetful to entertain strangers: for thereby some have entertained angels unawares." - Hebrews 13:2*

playing out in my own life on a smaller scale. In the Old Testament, Elijah's servant, who had been so fearful of the impending army they faced, was told, "Fear not: for they that be with us are more than they that be with them" (2 Kings 6:16). Then he saw "the mountain was full of horses and chariots of fire round about" coming to their aid (2 Kings 6:17). I felt the same thing was happening on our behalf, as our room filled with an unseen army of angels fighting for Lexi's very life.

As I prepared to return home for the night, I leaned down to give Lexi a parting kiss. Then I gently brushed a strand of blonde hair away from her eyes and tucked it behind her ear. Stroking her arm, I leaned forward and whispered that I loved her. Her eyes were not open, but I believed she could hear me. I gave her one more glance before I left.

As I began my exit, I felt strength leave me. Just stepping outside of her room, there was a tangible difference in the spirit that I felt, and, as a result, I felt alone and vulnerable. I prayed to my Heavenly Father that His Spirit would stay with me so that I could maintain the same spiritual high that I had while at Lexi's side. I didn't want to walk outside into the world, as it felt almost as if I was leaving heaven. However when I exited the hospital, the noise of the cars, coupled with the business of life, was a rude awakening. I was in the real world again.

The lingering daylight vanished, as the shadows had long since stole across the valley, my car barely visible in the darkness. I pleaded with the Lord to know how I might stay in a state of comfort and peace. I needed His "angels round about [me] to bear [me] up" (D&C 84:88). After I finished my prayer, these words came immediately to my mind: "Marcia, look up." I did accordingly, and with the moon illuminating the sky, I saw right in front of me the most stunning array of clouds in the heavens.

It was if God was saying to me, "I'm right here. I won't leave you. You are mine. I know you, and I am aware of what you are going through. '[I am] with you, while ye be with [Me]; and if ye seek [Me], [I] will be found of you' (2 Chronicles 15:2)."

His voice whispered to me that His presence would be with me and that these clouds were to show

> *"Did not our heart burn within us, while he talked with us by the way...?" - Luke 24:32*

His marvelous love for me. I drew in a breath as a rush of

courage surged though me. My eyes started to tear, and I was filled with unspeakable joy as a heavenly light distilled upon my soul. And I was reminded of the children of Israel when "the Lord went before them by day in a pillar of a cloud, to lead them the way" (Exodus 13:21). I, too, had received a glimpse into heaven through the lingering brilliance of the clouds.

The Lord has also taught others this concept of "looking up. "For instance, He taught the children of Israel through Moses to look up to "a fiery serpent...upon a pole: and...every one that [was] bitten, when he [looked] upon it,[lived]" (Numbers 21:8). But in Alma we learn that some would not look. Why is that? It is because "they did not believe that it would heal them" (Alma 33:20). Yet, the Lord promises us that if we do "cast about [our] eyes...and begin to believe in the Son of God...then [will] God grant unto [us] that [our] burdens may be light" (Alma 33:21-23). What a small thing we are asked to do in order for our burdens to be lifted.

I continued to watch the clouds as I drove home, and the feeling of peace persisted. I became lost in thought, pondering on God's mercy given to me. The stillness of the night caused me to pause and reverently feel His arms encircling me in His love.

As I continued to drive back and forth between home and the hospital each day, the first thing I would do in the first

> *"...I will go before your face. I will be on your right hand and on your left, and my Spirit shall be in your hearts, and mine angels round about you, to bear you up." - D&C 84:88*

golden glow of dawn was to look up at the sky to see the wonderment of the clouds. There seemed to be a reverence and a hush over the city when I focused on looking up. I felt protected from outside influences in its stillness. I felt the Lord speaking to me, "Marcia, look what kind of formation I made for you today. Isn't that beautiful? I will be with you through this trial every step of the way. You just need to keep looking up." I found I couldn't wait to see what God had created for me each morning as my love for Him deepened.

I still can't go outside or get into my car without first admiring the clouds. Often as I look up at the sky above me, the grandeur of the heavens moves me to tears of gratitude and takes my breath away. No matter where we are, God has a way of showing us that He is near, if we will just look up.

CHAPTER THIRTEEN

THE MIRACLE THAT COMES THROUGH FASTING

"Therefore also now, saith the Lord, turn ye even to me with all your heart, and with fasting..." - Joel 2:12

I love the scripture found in Doctrine and Covenants which says, "Draw near unto me and I will draw near unto you; seek me diligently and ye shall find me; ask, and ye shall receive; knock, and it shall be opened unto you" (88:63).It teaches us that God is always ready to help us. However the key is whether or not we will invite Him in. I found that this particular scripture had great relevance as I prayed and fasted for Lexi.

Fasting hasn't always been easy for me. Many times I have fasted and found myself counting down the hours until I was able to eat again. However, in my anguish, fasting was a welcome reprieve from the distress I was experiencing. Food actually became a burden. As each day passed without eating, I could sense I was becoming more receptive to the promptings of the Holy Ghost and learning the mind and will of God as spirit spoke to spirit. Generally, our church leaders recommend not fasting too frequently or for excessive periods of time. However, in my grief, I found myself truly unable to eat, so I chose to continue fasting.

My cute son Tanner was worried about me because of the stress, heartache, and sleepless nights I had faced and was continuing to confront. He also noticed that no food had been brought to me from the waiting room. He was very perceptive because no No one else had realized I had not eaten for days since each member of my family was only with me sporadically due to the limited number of people allowed in Lexi's room.

"Mom," he told me, "if you don't eat something, you will collapse and have to be admitted to the hospital yourself. Then we will have to take care of you as well as Lexi.

You have GOT to eat! Really, Mom...you do. I'm going to go get some food for you right now."

I was touched by his perceptiveness and thoughtfulness. "Tan, I'm ok. I really am," I explained. "I'm not hungry, and I can feel the Lord fortifying me. I promise I will eat if my body needs to, but right now I am fine. I don't know how... but I am." Truly, I had felt a power beyond my own strengthening me, and it was a marvelous spiritual experience.

But Tanner was relentless, and on Saturday morning he came in again. "OK, Mom," he said, "I'm not going to let you do this any longer. I'm bringing you some food."

I had no desire for food, but I could tell he was not going to give this up, so I said, "OK Tan, I'll eat, but please give me until noon?" I said this to pacify him because I didn't think he would remember to come back.

But just like clockwork, he appeared in my room at twelve o'clock with a plate of food. "You promised mom," he reminded me and handed me a plate overflowing with an assortment of food.

Despite his kindness and my desire not to offend him, I couldn't bring myself to eat quite yet. I looked at him rather sheepishly. "I know I promised, but can you just give me a few more hours before I eat?"

Sensing my yearnings to fast, he agreed to wait, but he was insistent we come up with another time. "Ok then what time? Two?"

I quickly agreed. "Yes," I promised, "by two o'clock I will be ready."

He looked at me sternly but kindly. "This time it's a promise, and you can't break it."

I knew exactly what time it was when a few hours later Tanner walked through the doorway with a new plate of food. He said firmly but lovingly, "Ok you gave your word. It's time to eat!"

He placed the food down by my chair and left the room. Just as he left, a doctor came in, so I slipped the meal behind some books to get it out of the way while the doctor talked to me. Not much more than a half hour went by when Tanner emerged again. His eyes scanned the room and quickly and saw the lunch was gone. He beamed, assuming I'd eaten the food, and excitedly praised me: "You ate it. Way to go. I'm so proud of you."

> *"Howbeit this kind goeth not out but by prayer and fasting."*
> *- Matthew 17:21*

For a minute our roles were reversed, and I was the child. I didn't have the heart to tell him I had not consumed any of it, but I couldn't lie either, so I slid back the stack of books revealing the hidden plate of food and sheepishly told him, "Sorry, Tan, I haven't taken a bite yet, but I will."

However, deep inside I knew that I couldn't, at least not yet...maybe tomorrow. Tanner didn't bother me again about the food. An understanding came to his heart that I needed to fast and that the Lord would take care of me. But Tanner's desire to look out for my physical welfare made me feel fortunate and cared for. It was the perfect preface to the Sabbath which would begin the next day, a day of community fasting and prayer for Lexi, in which every heart would be as one.

Fasting is a commandment that has been practiced by God's people throughout time. An example from the Book of Mormon is the sons of Mosiah as they prepared for their missionary labors among the wicked Lamanites. They didn't just pray for blessings but also "fasted much" (Alma 17:9). Why is that? Alma explains it is so "the Lord would grant unto them a portion of his Spirit to go with them and abide with them, that they might be an instrument in the hands of God... [and] the Lord did visit them with his Spirit, and said unto them: Be comforted. And they were comforted" (Alma 17:9-10).

I don't think it was a coincidence that the Sunday after Lexi's accident was a fast Sunday[19] for our church. I believe it was another act of charity from God. At a time of such unbearable grief, the Lord could not have given me a greater support than to have solace through fasting. I knew in my heart that this was a pivotal day in Lexi's progress. That day thousands of people fasted for Lexi, including her friends, extended family, neighbors, children, and people she had never met from all over the world. Lexi's LDS bishop[20]at BYU even

---

[19]Besides going without food and water on fast Sunday, our congregation meets together to bear testimony of God and the Savior the first Sunday of every month

[20]Leader of her local ward, or congregation

[21] A stake is a group of congregations or wards in the LDS Church, consisting of about three thousand to five thousand church members. A Stake President presides over a stake and is responsible for the physical and spiritual welfare of the members. It is not a paid position. (lds.org).

organized a continuous fast on the night of the accident with her ward. Every day until Sunday night, he arranged to have a several hundred people taking turns fasting for her.

Our neighborhood bishop also called and told us that the stake president[21] had asked the entire stake to fast for Lexi. He also mentioned that our ward wanted to have a special prayer for her at the end of fast and testimony meeting. After hearing this, I was overwhelmed with gratitude but also felt strongly that the bishop should have the entire congregation kneel down for that prayer instead of sitting on the pews. I felt it needed to be done this way as we approached the God of heaven, asking for such an incredible miracle. Doug, didn't feel like he should bother the bishop with this request, but with my insistence, he was kind enough to call our bishop back to ask him. After the bishop consulted with a member of the stake presidency, they decided it would be appropriate.

Many of our friends and neighbors who went to that meeting said they could feel the presence of angels when they entered the chapel. Others told me that they had never been to a more sacred church meeting in their entire lives. Even little children stood up and bore testimony that Lexi would be healed! It seemed the whole community was ablaze with the fire of faith and testimony that if they did their part, Lexi could be healed.

As our family prayed and fasted for Lexi on that Sunday, we also had the most spiritual uplifting day. The family went to church that morning, while I stayed with Lexi. A few of my children bore their testimonies of the Savior and eternal families,

> 'Verily my Sabbaths ye shall keep: for it is a sign between me and you..that ye may know that I am the Lord that doth sanctify you." - Exo. 31:13

which was the perfect start for the incredible spiritual experiences to follow. While we fasted, prayed, and read the scriptures during the day, we felt God especially near us. Despite being in a hospital setting, all the girls in our family had managed to find dresses to wear and the men suits, bringing an added spirit of reverence to the Sabbath. Never in my life have I felt the living waters of Jesus Christ flow so abundantly into the recesses of my being as I did that fast Sunday.

Throughout the day, the family continued their usual rotation of two people alternating in and out of the room at a time to see Lexi. However, at about four o'clock, family members began coming in Lexi's room without waiting for the other family members to leave. It was as if the Spirit was drawing us to be there together.

The Miracle That Comes Through Fasting

While I was standing next to Lexi, holding her hand, she gently blinked opened her eyes for the first time and kept them open. Even though they had taken her off the sedation medication, she still hadn't opened her eyes longer than a minute or two before closing them again. I

> *"Fear ye not, stand still and see the salvation of the Lord, which he will shew to you to day:... The Lord shall fight for you."*
> *- Exo.14:13-14*

could not remove my gaze from her face. I suggested that we sing some hymns to her, sensing that music would be the cure. Everyone agreed, and we sang "Be Still My Soul," "Abide with Me!," "I Know That My Redeemer Lives," and other hymns that we loved and knew would bring peace to Lexi.

We were surprised that after every song we sang, her eyes remained wide open, watching our every move. So we continued to sing. As this was happening, Lexi's sister Kelsi raced outside of the room to gather the few stragglers who were still in the waiting area and notified them to come and see Lexi opening her eyes. As we huddled together in that small ICU room, we were blessed through God's benevolence that not one member of the hospital staff asked us to leave. This was remarkable because we have such a large family. As each family member entered the room, Lexi gingerly raised her hand and waved to them. My eyes blinked, tears pooling and spilling onto the floor as we started to see this miracle unfold before our eyes. We sang for nearly an hour and, as we did, the Spirit entered the room in greater abundance. It was as if we were experiencing a piece of heaven.

As we sang, Lexi slowly moved her gaze from one person to the next until she had looked at every person in the room. At that moment, we felt that she knew who we were and that she comprehended the situation. She even tried to touch her sister Shae with her toes when she saw her at the end of her bed. We also knew that family on the other side of the veil had joined us in the room. It seemed even "the mountains [shouted] for joy...and the seas and dry lands [told] the wonders of [our] Eternal King. And...the sun, moon, and the morning stars [sang with us], and...all the sons of God [shouted] for joy"(D&C 128: 23; see also Job 38:7). Prior to this moment, I had never felt such incredible love for Lexi, for my family, and especially for the Lord.

Then after singing, the most remarkable, the most unforgettable thing happened. With every eye locked on Lexi, she hand-signed, "I love you," moving her outstretched arm around in a circle to let each of us see. Then she repeated the sign again with her other hand in the opposite direction. A hush fell over the room. My heart quickened, hardly daring to breathe, for we felt we were on hallowed ground. Besides the sniffs and hiccups caused by tears, silence penetrated the space. The Spirit whispered to us that we were literally eye witnesses to a miracle.

Tears flowed freely, and God's graciousness overwhelmed us. The strength of His love had been felt from the tops of our heads to the bottom of our soles. God had heard our pleas and accepted our fast. By His power we felt and saw with our own eyes that he brought our daughter and sister, Lexi, back to life.

How was it possible? I was still trying to take it all in and to fully comprehend what had just taken place. She was completely aware of everyone around her when only an hour ago she was still in a coma like state. Our "hearts were swollen with joy, unto the gushing out of many tears, because of the great goodness of God" (3 Nephi 4:33).My daughter-in-law Mandy summed it up well when she wrote,

> *"Know ye not that ye are in the hands of God? Know ye not that he hath all power..?" - Mormon 5:23*

"The spirit was so powerful and seemed to coat every inch of the room. I literally felt it radiate through my entire body."

After Lexi signed, "I love you," she reached her hand up to Parker who was standing closest to her. He took her hand and held it for a minute before she let go and reached for the person standing next to him. She continued reaching out her hand until she had grasped the hand of each family member individually. It was as if she wanted each of us know of her love for us. The silence in the room deepened, and we marveled over the wonder we had experienced. No one wanted to leave the sweetness of the room, but because of the hospital policy, the family exited, wrapped in a newness of life. As each person left, Lexi gave a slight smile and waved good-bye. We learned the truth of Isaiah's promise that after we fast then "thou shalt call, and the Lord shall answer; and then thou shalt cry, and he shall say, Here I am" (Isaiah 58:9).

I've always pondered how it would feel to have lived in Christ's day and to see His miracles. But through this experience my soul burned bright with the knowledge that I had personally seen Christ's power. Joshua's words had literally been fulfilled to us when he wrote, "Sanctify yourselves: for...the Lord will do wonders among you" (Joshua 3:5). And we "did rejoice, and [our] whole [hearts were] filled, because of the things which [we] had seen, yea, which the Lord had shown unto [us]" (1 Nephi 1:15). Our

God is indeed a God of miracles. Jesus had loosened the bands of death, and I felt to shout praises to heaven.

The next day my niece Angela told me about her daughters, Mary and Emma, who were just four and eight years old. She and her husband told them on that particular Sunday that their family was going to hold a fast for Lexi. They also explained that fasting meant to sacrifice food and water in order to call down a blessing from heaven. After learning this, Emma and Mary decided that they wanted to fast for the first time with their parents. Later

> *Jesus said to the children, "Blessed are ye because of your faith. And now behold, my joy is full. And when he had said these words, he wept." - 3 Nephi 17:20-21*

that evening, after they had completed their fast, the family read the post on the "Pray for Lexi" Facebook page that shared how Lexi had awoken from her coma that evening. After reading about the amazing miracle that had just happened, Mary and Emma were astonished. Mary turned to her mom and whispered, "I didn't know a little kid, like me, could help a big person."

Likewise, our hearts were touched as we were told of the many children and adults from different parts of the world who fasted for Lexi and who took it upon themselves to help bear our burden. We were humbled by their boldness, their believing hearts, and their connection to heaven. The glow of their testimonies is best described by the scripture, "If thou canst believe, all things are possible" (Mark 9:23). The Spirit also confirmed to them that Lexi's miracle was a result of their

 fasting and their faith in the tender mercies of a loving God.

After this amazing miracle, we assumed that this was the end of our trial, for our Lexi had been brought back to us. Yet we would soon find out that the Lord wanted to teach our family many other lessons. We would discover how many more deep rivers we needed to wade through in order to refine our characters.

CHAPTER FOURTEEN

THE MIRACLE TO ACCEPT OUR TRIALS

"The Lord is my rock, and my fortress, and my deliverer; The God of my rock; in him will I trust: he is my shield, and the horn of my salvation, my high tower, and my refuge, my saviour..." - 2 Samuel 22:2-3

My son McKay shared some of his thoughts after Lexi came out of the coma. He wrote:

"We have followed Lexi's story in the media with amazement as it has caught not just local, but also worldwide interest. Articles about her have been published in faraway places like Nigeria, Brazil, and the UK. As I read these articles, I have been drawn to the comments of the readers. I wondered if other people would also believe the miracle. By and large, the comments were positive and supportive; however, there was also a common thread in which people expressed a very thoughtful concern for others who have suffered and haven't recovered. Their question in a nutshell is, "What of those whose pleas to God have seemingly gone unanswered? If God is a caring, loving God, wouldn't He love them like He loves Lexi?"

I have pondered this very real and genuine concern and wanted to share what I have learned. First, I don't presume to know why God chooses to heal and bless some while letting others suffer tremendously. It is indeed hard to fathom how a caring, loving God would permit His children to experience pain and heartache. But to all those who have watched others suffer or suffered themselves and wonder why God allowed it, I would direct them to our Exemplar and Savior, Jesus Christ. Just as we are allowed to suffer, He whom God called his "Beloved Son," was allowed to suffer more than anyone who has ever walked the face of the earth. Christ describes His own suffering in this way: "how exquisite you know not, yea, how hard to bear you know not" (D&C 19:15).

It appears that even Christ himself didn't completely understand the need for all the pain that lay ahead of Him as he knelt in the Garden of Gethsemane and petitioned His Father to "remove this cup" (Luke 22:42). Did this mean that Christ was unloved by His Father? No! He lived and experienced His Father's love almost every moment of His life and sought every day to teach all of us exactly what this pure love was and how to achieve it.

Yet, God did have His reasons to allow such travail and agony: through Christ's suffering, He atoned for our sins. Additionally, the prophet Alma testified, "I do know that whosoever shall put their trust in God shall be supported in their trials, and their troubles, and their afflictions..." (Alma 36:3). Notice that he didn't say that the trials would be removed or taken away but that we would be supported through them. And we saw this take place for our family. When Lexi was in the coma, our family put our trust in God, and we received support! We received it in the form of comfort and peace through our Savior. We were able to be consoled by Christ because He had suffered and experienced our pain; therefore He knew how to console us in our sorrows: "And he shall go forth, suffering pains and afflictions and temptations of every kind...that he may know according to the flesh how to succor his people according to their infirmities" (Alma 7:11-12).

Many of the trials and pain we experience is the result of living in an imperfect world and is not caused by God. But just as our Savior, Jesus Christ, is able to lift and strengthen us in our infirmities because of the afflictions that He bore, we can also become more capable of lifting others when we go through trials and tribulations. Moreover, God shows His love to us by lifting us and supporting us through our trials. He often accomplishes this through the means of other people who have also suffered or gone through similar trials and therefore can offer empathy, encouragement, and a shoulder to lean on. I ultimately believe that Lexi was healed so she can be the means of showing the goodness of God to others. However, even if she had not been made whole, I know that we would have still received His support and peace and eventually my family could and would have been healed through His marvelous gift!"

Like my son McKay, my heart has also gone out to those who have not had prayers answered as directly as our prayers for Lexi were. Yet, I feel I can understand a little of what some are going through because our oldest daughter, Shae, has not been healed of her afflictions. She was born with multiple disabilities. She is deaf, has cerebral palsy, and some mental deficiencies. And despite our prayers, she continues to struggle with these challenges.

> *"Now no chastening for the present seemeth to be joyous, but grievous: nevertheless afterward it yieldeth the peaceable fruit of righteousness..."* - Heb. 12:11.

Lexi has seen firsthand how lonely life can be when your body doesn't work properly, especially if that person is deaf and isolated from the hearing world, so learning sign language was extremely important to Lexi. Even though she

learned sign language at home, she wanted to be more proficient at it. Her high school didn't offer a sign language class and her principal refused to add it, but Lexi was undeterred and asked any interested students to sign a petition to get the class included in the curriculum. Because of the overwhelming amount of signatures, the principal's heart was swayed and the class was added. From this experience, Lexi's American Sign Language skills significantly improved, and this helped to deepen her relationship with her sister.

Although Lexi was 15 years younger than Shae, it became apparent to Lexi at an early age that Shae didn't have any friends besides her family. Like the rest of her siblings, Lexi colored pictures and played simple games with her and helped to feed and dress her. Shae would then lovingly pat Lexi's head or sign "I love you." Because of Shae's limitations, many times she would take her frustrations out on the family. Sometimes she would rip out chunks of Lexi's blonde hair or bite or hit her. Despite the sting of Shae's anger, Lex was quick to forgive.

When Shae was born, our minds anguished, thinking her life would be plagued by scorn and ridicule by her classmates and others. We were rightly concerned that her life would be difficult. But over the years, we have learned to trust in the Lord, knowing He knows what is best for us. He listens to our prayers even when those petitions aren't answered the

way *we* want. Looking back, we have gained wisdom from the trials that have been a part of our lives and have come to recognize that our prayers were unanswered not because God does not love us but because He trusts us to be faithful in the midst of our challenges.

In order for our family to be reminded of this principle--to trust in the Lord's wisdom daily - we have three words stenciled above the doorway in our living room: *But if not.* These words come from a scriptural account in Daniel.

Nebuchadnezzar had constructed a great image and commanded the people that "at what time ye hear the sound of the . . . musick, ye fall down and worship the golden image.... And whoso falleth not down and worshippeth shall the same hour be cast into the midst of a burning fiery furnace....Therefore at that time, when all the people heard the sound...of musick...all the people...fell down and worshipped the golden image" (Daniel 3:5-7). However, three young men-- Shadrach, Meshach, and Abed-nego--were steadfast and immovable in their beliefs and remained standing. When they were brought before the king, he demanded, "And who is that God that shall deliver you out of my hands?" (Daniel 3:15).

The faith of these young men shone bright in their resolved response: "If it be so, our God whom we serve is able to deliver us from the burning fiery furnace, and he will deliver us out of thy hand, O king. **But if not**, be it known unto thee, O king, that we will not serve thy gods, nor worship the golden image which thou hast set up" (Daniel 3:17- 18). They were then bound, fully clothed, and thrown into the flames.

However, as the king looked into the flames, he saw that they walked freely, unbound and unhurt, and that a fourth person was with them. Then they came forth from the furnace with their hair and clothing untouched. Not even "the smell of fire had passed on them" (Daniel 3:27).

> *"...he will deliver us out of thy hand, O king. But if not...we will not serve thy gods." - Dan.3:17-18.*

Can we have faith in God's plan for us like Shadrach, Meshach, and Abed-nego even if it means our reward won't come to us in this life? Elder Dennis E. Simmons counseled that, like them, we should say, "Our God will deliver us from ridicule and persecution, *but if not*....Our God will deliver us from sickness and disease, *but if not*....He will deliver us from loneliness, depression, or fear, *but if not*... . He will make sure that we are loved and recognized, *but if not*....We will receive a perfect companion and righteous and obedient children, *but if not*.... *we will trust in the Lord*" ("But If Not...," April 2004).

I believe that the three virtuous women in the book of Abraham who would not bow down to worship gods of wood or of stone, but "... were killed upon (the) altar" (Abraham 1:11), said in their hearts the words of faith that Shadrach, Meshach and Abednego declared. We believe our God will save us, but if not... we will trust God. I wish more people knew of the faith and sacrifice of these three virgins. To remember that being obedient doesn't always save us from heart ache, tests, and in their case, even death.

Some of the trials we endure in life can last for years and we may wonder if they will ever be lifted from us. Sometimes when we cry out for help we may question if our pleadings are landing on deaf ears. The prophet Nephi must have felt this way when the record states he did "cry much unto the Lord...because of the anger of [his] brethren" (2 Nephi 5:1). These weren't just casual prayers as the wording of this scripture seems to indicate an intense pleading to the Lord to soften his brothers' hearts. How did the Lord answer Nephi's prayer? Were his brothers' hardened hearts dissolved into love, allowing them to show kindness to Nephi and his family? The next verse explains that "their anger did increase against [Nephi] insomuch that they did seek to take away [his] life" (2 Nephi 5:2).

I'm sure many of us can relate to having a prayer answered in this manner, where the very thing that we are praying to be relieved of becomes even harder to bear. Likewise the answers to our prayers can take us in different directions than we desire. This happened for Nephi who, in response to his prayer, was commanded by God to take his family into the wilderness. This was in stark contrast to what Nephi had been praying for. I'm sure he thought about his parents, Lehi and Sariah, and how they would have wanted the family to stay together. This was not the answer that he was seeking.

But, like Nephi, can we do anything less than to follow God's counsel and enter our own unknown wildernesses? I have learned that as I follow God's instructions, He always leads me from the darkest hour of night into the dawn of His morning light. Each time I have trusted and obeyed, my faith has grown stronger, and I have been reminded that God sees the big picture, while I only see the here and now.

CHAPTER FIFTEEN

THE MIRACLE THAT CHRIST HEALS THE BROKEN HEARTED

"And forgive us our debts as we forgive our debtors." - Matthew 6:12

On Monday, March 3rd, five days after the accident, I arrived back at the hospital early in the morning. My son Tanner and his wife Mandy had stayed the night with Lexi, and I finally felt well rested after having my first peaceful sleep since the accident. When I came into Lexi's room, Tanner and Mandy were anxiously waiting for me.

"Mom, you would not believe what was delivered to Lexi's room last night," Tanner announced, suddenly thoughtful.

Mandy hurried across the room and picked up an envelope from the table and handed it to me. "It's from the driver of the car that had hit Lexi," she said in a seemingly reverent voice. "A nurse brought it to our room late last night."

My heart sank when I saw the letter because up until this point our family had not been able to find or contact the driver to let him know that we were not angry and didn't hold him responsible. I felt it was our duty to reach out to him and not the other way around, knowing he would have been scared to reach out to us. I felt horrible knowing he had suffered needlessly, when he was also in desperate need of support. I felt our family should have done more to contact him.

I opened the folded up piece of paper and began reading. In the letter he penned, "I want you to know how heartbroken and sorrowful I feel about what has happened to Lexi. My heart just aches every single day knowing what has happened to such an amazing daughter, sister, and friend." He continued, since the accident I have been endlessly fasting and praying for miracles to take

> *"He hath sent me to heal the brokenhearted."*
> *- Luke 4:18.*

place on her behalf. I have felt on a very personal level the amount of love God has for Lexi and the rest of your family. With each update on Lexi's condition I am humbled by your unity and faith in Jesus Christ and his ability to work miracles in our lives. With all the conviction of my soul I want you to know how sorry I feel that this accident took place and I pray you have felt my prayers pleading with our Father in Heaven to comfort Lexi and to comfort all of you during this difficult time. I will continue to pray for Lexi and the entire Hansen family and to comfort your family."

My heart ached for him as I read of the sorrow and pain that he had suffered, especially when reading the words he wrote expressing how "In my own life I take pride in, and feel so much joy in making people around me feel good but to know the sadness and grief that has come from this accident has shaken me to the very core." Although it was a different type of grief than what we were experiencing, I'm sure he cried out that first night, as we did, "O God, where art thou? And where is the pavilion that covereth thy hiding place? How long shall thy hand be stayed...?" (D&C 121:1-2). Oh, how I felt for him! I thought about how if this had been one of my own sons, I would have wanted a kind and tender person reaching out to him.

I could tell by his letter that he also had a strong foundation in the Lord. One of the last things he wrote was very powerful: "I know that through our Savior Jesus Christ, we can ALL be healed." I love how he said "we," knowing that our family's hearts needed to be healed in addition to Lexi's body. But in a much larger scope, his words also remind us that no matter what struggle we are going through in life, it is only the Savior that can change us.

Later he expressed to me how reading the Facebook page we had set up for Lexi had only made his grief worse. As he read about her life, he realized he had hit a girl who was not only loved and respected by many, but who was also devoted to God. She was good, kind, and loving, and he was the one responsible for potentially taking her life.

At the bottom of the letter, he signed his name, Karson, and left his phone number and email address. The night

before, Mandy had the impression that she should send him an email right away to let him know that our family had been praying and fasting for him in addition to Lexi. I'm sure Karson had been extremely nervous sending the letter, not knowing how it would be received. And he had taken a leap of faith by leaving his name and number at the end.

After I finished reading the letter, it was just barely 6:00 a.m., so I decided it was still too early to call him. I waited impatiently until about 7:30 a.m., but when I called, no one picked up the phone. I waited another half hour and called again, yet there was still no answer. This time I decided to leave a voice mail.

In the message, I let Karson know that we were not upset with him. I told him accidents just happen and that I believed this misfortune had

> "Now therefore, be not grieved, nor angry with [yourself]...for God did send [you]...to preserve life...by a great deliverance." - Genesis 45:5, 7

happened for a reason. I let him know that I believed this was all part of God's plan, as our community and the world were hungering for knowledge that God still answers prayers. I believed we all needed to be part of a miracle to strengthen our faith and to be reminded that God is still a God of miracles. I expressed to him how sorry I was for the anguish he was experiencing, and that I knew he was chosen for his strength of character to go through this tragedy--to be the catalyst to bring about the love that seemed to be overflowing in the community. I then asked him if he would meet us in the hospital waiting room to have dinner together that night. I expressed again how sorry I was for the pain he must be going through and hung up.

With all things considered, I didn't think he would call me back, so I waited another hour and called again. This time he answered the phone, and I reiterated what I had said previously in my voice mail. He told me he thought it was probably me when I had called the first time, but he had been too frightened to answer until after I had left the message. And he expressed his willingness to meet us for dinner that evening.

That night was the first time I had gone out into the waiting room since the accident, but I felt I needed to be there to let Karson know of my love for him. My son Tanner thoughtfully waited for him by the elevator doors and then led him over to where our family was anticipating his arrival.

Karson entered the foyer with fear and trepidation. He arrived dressed in a suit and tie, carrying with him a bouquet of flowers for Lexi and a box of gourmet cupcakes for the family. I

> "I have seen thy tears, I will heal thee."
> - 2 Kgs. 20:5

jumped to my feet to greet him and gave him a big hug. He felt like family from the first time I saw him. He fit right in. I could tell from his countenance that he was a good person. He was, of course, extremely nervous and hesitant. In fact, when I invited him to sit down and eat with us, he was candid in his reply: "I'm too nervous, there is no way I could eat anything," his voice strained with emotion. His body stiff, he shifted his weight, looking uncomfortable. His eyes seemed to reveal a helplessness, a longing to go back in time.

After introducing him to the family, I jokingly asked him, "Ok now I hope you remembered everyone's names." Although we have nine children, there were 21 of us together when counting the grandkids. Yet, surprisingly, he actually remembered quite a few names.

After the introductions, Karson sat down and talked to my children while I hurried back to be with Lexi. A great relief

washed over him as he was able to tell his side of the story and what he went through that night, seeing Lexi's lifeless body lying on the pavement. He expressed to them the horror he felt realizing he might have killed her. He said he took pride in and felt so much joy in making people around him feel good and had always tried to lead a good life. To know that he could have caused so much grief and sorrow was something he couldn't bear. He reiterated that he would never, ever hurt anyone intentionally.

Karson had not been speeding the night when his car hit Lexi, but the way in which the three way intersection was designed made it difficult for him to see her until she was directly in front of him. We also found out that the intersection was poorly lit that evening.

In fact, a few nights after the accident two police officers came to the hospital to inform us of the details that had transpired that evening. They told us that there were only three lights working in that vicinity despite the fact that it was dusk. The officers also mentioned to us that there had been several other accidents at that same location in recent years, yet when they had approached city leaders about fixing the problem, their pleas were met with silence. The police were hoping that with Lexi's accident that now the city would take note and do something.

While Karson visited with the family, he also told of a tender mercy he was given the night of the accident when he went to talk to a leader in his church. Unbeknownst to him, that man had also hit someone in his youth who had died from her injuries. Of all the people Karson could have gone to for comfort and counsel, the Lord placed him directly across from a man that could truly understand his pain and exactly what he was going through.

> *...the tender mercies of the Lord are over all those whom he hath chosen, because of their faith, to make them mighty even unto the power of deliverance."* - *1 Nep. 1:20*

That night, our new friend, Karson, reminded me of Joshua in the scriptures, as Joshua exhorts us many times "to be strong and of a good courage" (see Joshua 1:6, 9, 18; 10:25). It took a lot of courage for Karson to not only come to dinner, but also to write the letter in the first place. Later he told us that his walk down the hospital corridors to the security station to deliver the letter was the longest and most difficult trek he'd ever made in his entire life.

A few days later after our first introduction, Karson visited me again at the hospital. This time when I stepped out of Lexi's room to greet him in the waiting room, he was not wearing a suit and tie but a pink shirt. It was like meeting a different person; his

> *"Hope of the righteous shall be gladness."* - *Prov. 10:28*

eyes were bright, his countenance dramatically changed to one filled with joy, happiness, and hope. That was the key: hope. He believed that his future could be bright, and he was no longer weighed down by this tragic incident. I could tell just by looking at his glowing smile that a burden had been lifted from his shoulders.

The only other time I left the ICU to visit with someone was the night I met with Karson's parents. I was told they were in the waiting room wanting to meet me. I felt compelled to talk with them as I had with Karson, knowing that their hearts needed healing as well.

They were waiting in a private area by Lexi's room; their earnest and solemn demeanor suggested to me they were overcome with grief, despair, and guilt over something that was not their fault or their son's fault. Sorrow filled their eyes and apprehensiveness showed clearly on their faces, wondering how they might be received. I stepped up to Karson's dad who was closest to me and gave him a big bear hug and then turned to his weeping mom, who stood with her head bowed. I embraced her and told her how sorry I was for their pain. Tears continued to flow down her cheeks as she responded in what seemed a sense of disbelief to what I had just said.

She looked at me and said with gentleness in her voice, "Here you are comforting us, and we are the ones that should be comforting you."

> *"And Esau ran to meet him, and embraced him and fell on his neck, and kissed him: and they wept." - Gen 33:4*

But I knew the reason I could reach out to them was not because of any greatness in my character. In fact, I could tell

159

immediately upon seeing them that they were righteous and exceptional individuals. I could be strong and at peace at that moment only because God had surrounded and blessed me with a multitude of angels who had strengthened me in countless ways during the previous week. Those angels helped me attain new heights that I couldn't have reached on my own. They purified my soul, enlarged my understanding, and healed my wounded heart.

I reaffirmed to them that I knew this was all part of Gods plan that I firmly believed God had chosen Karson to go through such adversity because of the goodness of his heart and his strength of testimony. Tears gathered in my eyes when I told them of the many miracles that had happened daily since the accident and of the attending angels at her side-- experiences I had not shared with anyone else besides my children, yet I felt strongly they needed to hear. It was a warm and emotional meeting between three hearts, each of which had been torn and broken yet were now being mended through the healing power of Christ's atonement.

CHAPTER SIXTEEN

THE MIRACLE TO PRESS ON WITH COURAGE

"Therefore, dearly beloved brethren, let us cheerfully do all things that lie in our power; and then may we stand still, with the utmost assurance, to see the salvation of God, and for his arm to be revealed." - D&C 123:17

After a day of rejoicing on Sunday, we were not prepared for the complications that set in after Lexi awoke from her coma. It was a bitter pill to swallow. It was a long and grueling day emotionally and physically. I had to remind myself that this was just part of life with its ups and downs. Our role was to continue to trust God through it all.

Lexi was extubated, meaning that she had shown enough improvement for her breathing tube to be removed. I was surprised and overjoyed that she was progressing quickly. The breathing tube was replaced with a breathing mask that was only needed every few hours. This was a big step! I was also glad the tube came out because it had been pressing against her swollen lip and had made a huge dent in her lip that I knew must be quite painful. Because of the impression the tube had left, her smile was always just a half smile for several weeks. And her vocal cords were scratched and swollen from the tube having been down her throat as well. My heart clenched with hurt as I sat and watched what she had to go through. I leaned forward and stroked her arm reassuringly.

She was able to answer some questions in a raspy, barely-audible whisper, but her voice was so quiet when she spoke, we couldn't always decipher what she wanted to say. It was frustrating because we wanted to know how much she comprehended mentally, but her speech was usually unintelligible. However, because she knew sign language, she was able to express her needs in that manner when she had the strength to do so, which wasn't often. One night when she was thirsty she signed "water," and later, when she was asked what her name was, she finger spelled "Lexi."

If all these problems were not bad enough, they informed me that she had also caught pneumonia in one lung and they were worried that it might spread to her other lung. The respiratory therapist came in every few hours with a big breathing mask that formed a mist which, when inhaled, helped her with her breathing difficulties. At other times the therapist would rotate the mask with a vest which served as a ventilator and helped to loosen the mucous that had settled in her lungs. It

162

would vibrate her rib cages and help to make her cough. As the phlegm loosened, they would suction it out which allowed her airways to clear and would, in turn, help her breathe better

".... the Lord gave, and the Lord hath taken away: blessed be the name of the Lord." - Job 1:21

Lexi hated this, of course, and would cry out in pain and try to grab the tube from the nurse's hands because it would irritate her throat until it became inflamed and raw. I grimaced and felt my knees go weak as I watched her suffer, but I willed my tears not to escape in order to be strong for her.

She seemed to do much better and endure the horror when I gently stroked her forehead with my finger over and over; it was the only thing that seemed to soothe her. That day and the next couple of days were some of the hardest for Lexi personally since she was out of the coma and could feel the pain from the accident, but we knew "in the strength of the Lord [she could] do all things" (Alma 20:4).

Right after one of these treatments, one of our favorite nurses came in and scolded me for having too many people and too much noise in Lexi's room. I turned around and stared at her. Could she really mean what she just said? I was surprised not only by her curt tone but also because I felt we had been obeying the rules, conversing mostly through whispers and allowing only two people in her room at one time. In fact at the exact moment when she came in, the only other person in the room besides me was my oldest son, McKay, who was reading his scriptures in the corner of the room.

I kindly asked the nurse to please be softer with her words, as there were angels in the room helping Lexi who would depart if there was contention. But her eyes narrowed, and she insisted that we weren't obeying the rules. I had no energy for a battle of wills and had to let it go. She had always been kind and cheerful, so I wondered what triggered the episode; maybe her supervisor had admonished her for allowing our entire family in Lexi's room to sing to her the night before.

Whether she had been reprimanded or was just having a bad day, I don't know, but as soon as she left the room, I broke into tears because of the negative spirit that was brought needlessly in the room. I had not cried like that at any other time since arriving at the hospital. It was like a dam had broken and there was no way to stop it. As I wept,

I was surprised to see Lexi extend her arm out to me, looking at me steadily. I didn't realize that she was awake and aware of what was happening around her. She couldn't talk, but managed to mouth, "Sorry, Mom." Her eyes said it all, and they pierced my soul with tenderness and love. I reached out and took hold of her hand, stifling my tears and forcing a smile for her sake.

When she drifted off to sleep, I sank back down in my chair, and my shoulders started to shake, tears coming afresh. I buried my face in my hands and sobbed uncontrollably for over an hour, until I had run out of tears and my eyes stung. My strength drained from me. I needed my daughter to heal, and I knew that the contention would delay her healing.

One nurse seeing me cry, sat down next to me stroking my back, telling me it would be alright. Her kindness was soothing. I'm sure part of the reason for the flood of tears was the release of tension that had built up over the past couple of days. I was spent from the emotionally exhausting whirlwind of the past week. I felt I had done well suppressing my feelings, yet the steady stream of tears found an escape at last. Sometimes I felt like "the battle was before and behind" (2 Chronicles 13:14) as I struggled with my concerns for Lexi and dealt with outside issues. Yet despite these hurdles, we still felt like "the wind did never cease to blow towards the promised land," (Ether 6:8) as Lexi continued to make baby steps to recovery.

The doctor came in soon after I stopped crying to check on Lexi. He pointed to me and asked her who I was. I was worried that she might not remember me. However, in the slightest of whispers, she barely made out the word, "Mom." The realization of what she had said hit me with power. I was elated. Moments like this helped bring brightness to long, tedious, and sometimes heart-wrenching days of despair. I couldn't help bending down to lightly kiss her forehead, pulling her blanket around her shoulders.

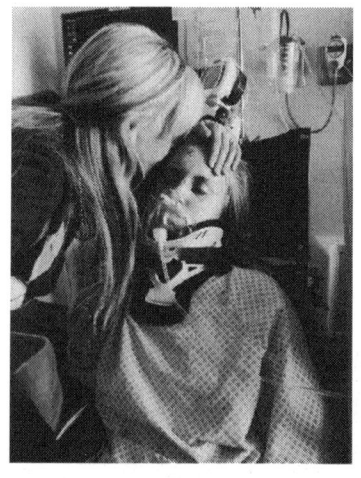

Before the doctor left he said with a compassionate smile, "She's a miracle, just remember that" as he lifted his head upwards in emphasis. Nodding my head, my hand found my heart, our eyes locked, and a testimony was shared.

Just then, Tanner cheerfully sauntered in and asked Lexi how Grandma and Grandpa were doing, referring to my parents who had passed

"...for the joy of the Lord is your strength." - Neh.8:10

away a few years before. I was half startled to see her open her eyes and give him a thumbs up.

Though her speech was slurred and not readily understandable, the next few days Lexi answered questions about her name, date of birth, where she was going to school, and about her siblings - and with eight siblings, that's no small task. During our rounds of questions, her brother JD threw in one of his own and said, "Who's your favorite brother?" Of course he thought she would say his name since he had asked the question, but Lexi in a scarcely-detectable voice mumbled,

"Parker," causing us to chuckle at J.D.'s expense. But we knew it was true; Lexi and Parker were closest in age, giving them a special bond.

While we were talking, I happened to glance over at Lex and noticed her fiddling with something. But because her back was towards me, I assumed she was playing with her hospital wristband. The doctors had restrained Lexi's arms while she was in the coma so she wouldn't reach up and take out her tubes. Within seconds however, a loud beeping noise invaded the space, interrupting the monotonous humming of machines.

I whirled around and leaped to my feet as a nurse dashed into the room. It was then that we saw Lexi had unscrewed the blood pressure cables. The nurse was astonished because she had never seen a restrained patient with the dexterity to undo such tiny screws. Lexi was not happy when the nurse pulled the restraints on Lexi's arms a little tighter so that she had less flexibility to harm herself.

I again touched the side of Lexi's forehead - one of the few unscathed places on her face - and tenderly brushed it with the tips of my fingers, soothing her back to sleep. She peered at me lovingly under her dark long lashes, smiling slightly, or maybe it was her eyes that let me know she would have smiled if she could have.

That week Lexi also got her catheter out, but she refused to go to the bathroom in a bedpan. It would take three people to pick her up and put her on a movable toilet by her bed. The first time I realized she would not use the bedpan, I was sitting in the corner of her room when, without warning, she sat straight up and swung her legs dangerously off the side of the bed. I leaped to my feet and grabbed her before she fell onto the floor, while frantically searching for the call button to get help.

I shudder to think what would have happened if I had not been in the room at that time because she was hooked up to several machines and could not even stand by herself. But in this instance, she seemed to have super-human strength. The rest of the day she would lay in bed, barely able to move her limbs, let alone pull herself into a sitting position. The nurse's jaw dropped when she reached the room and saw Lexi sitting up, legs draped over the side of the bed. We were both grateful a crisis had been averted.

The days blended together that week. On one afternoon, I had just stepped outside the room to talk with a visitor when Lexi pulled her feeding tube part way out. When I came back in, creamy white liquid coming out of her nose which caused her to have a coughing

> *"Be strong and of a good courage; be not afraid ...for the Lord thy God is with thee."*
> *- Joshua 1:9.*

attack. I soon realized that the fluid was formula that had escaped from the feeding tube and was now going down her throat. Lexi winced in pain, tears streaking down her cheeks when the nurse had to pull out the feeding tube the rest of the way. I reached for her hand, squeezing it tight to help her deal with the pain and bit my lower lip so I would not cry. It was difficult to watch her suffer daily on top of everything she'd already gone through.

Despite these challenges, it was satisfying to see Lexi move around more considering that she had been lying motionless while in a coma, and I felt a growing sense of comfort. One day that week, she lifted her left leg up and flopped it back down on the bed several times in a row. Her eyes were closed, but in an attempt to get her to move her limbs on her right side, I said, "Wow, Lex, you can move your left leg so high. Can you move your right leg too?"

I was surprised and delighted when she lifted her right leg barely off the sheet because I didn't think she was even listening to me. Hoping to get more movement out of her, I continued, "That was pretty good Lex, but do you think you can you lift your right leg even higher?" And with that, she lifted her leg up so hard she flung it clear over the side of the bed, her eyes still closed. I dove to that side of the bed and put her leg back, glad that she had not fallen off the bed before I reached her. She always kept us smiling despite the seriousness of the situation.

By the end of the week, Lexi was not only able to wiggle her toes, lift her legs up, and stick out her tongue on command, but her therapists also got her out of bed and had her stand - albeit with a lot of assistance. Her legs were wobbly and awkward as she was helped to her feet. It took a great deal of effort for her to lock her knees in place so that she could stand up straight. With two physical therapists on either side holding her up, she took a couple steps forward. One therapist would slide Lexi's left foot forward and then the other therapist would push her right foot. Her legs continued to buckle, but they managed to hold her steady, keeping a firm grip on her arms, legs, and torso.

After walking like this for a few feet, Lexi was asked if she wanted to go back to bed, but she pointed forward, indicating that she wanted to keep practicing. Her determination showed on her face. These five-minute exercises would wear her out for the rest of the day, so we knew it was going to be a long and painful process for her to regain her abilities. But she was "willing to submit to all the things which the Lord [saw] fit to inflict upon [her]" (Mosiah 3:19).

At one point to break things up a bit, Cassidy asked Lexi if she wanted to have a thumb war and begin moving her thumb back and forth and singing. The instant she did this,

Lexi started wiggling her thumb back and forth,
then unexpectedly smashed Cassidy's thumb down so fiercely
that Cassidy couldn't get out of her strong grip. Lexi was
surging back to her former self with renewed vigor.

Fortunately there was respite on occasion from the
rigors of hospital life. On
Wednesday, a week after the
accident, one of my children had
allowed my good friend to come
into the ICU just outside Lexi's

> *The Lord is good, a strong hold in the day of trouble; and he knoweth them that trust in him." - Nahum 1:7*

room so I could say hi to her. We exchanged embraces, visited
for a moment, and then I allowed her to come inside to see
Lexi for a brief moment.

Just as she stepped through the doorway, Lexi's speech
therapist entered and asked me who my guest was. For 30 years
I have referred to her as my sister, since most people have
assumed we are because she looks so much like me. I told the
therapist that she was my sister, partly out of habit and also
because I didn't want to get in trouble for having someone in
her room that was not a family member.

The therapist walked over to Lexi to start her therapy
and the first question she asked as she pointed to my friend
was, "Is that your aunt?"

Luckily Lexi couldn't talk, but she nodded a definite

"No." My two daughters in the room and I tried not to giggle. My friend averted the nurse's eyes and promptly slipped from the room while I distracted the therapist. The therapist thought Lexi's memory wasn't good, but we knew better.

This week had opened a door to suffering that would have challenged the very bravest soul. Yet Lexi was courageous. Her tenacity caused me to marvel. Her hope never faltered or melted away. My eyes burned, tears springing to my eyes as I sat by her side, minute after minute, hour after hour seeing first hand that nothing could mask the throbbing pain she was called to bear. I too needed courage. I would not allow myself to ever feel distant from God's promises to Lexi. And deep within, I knew that I could continue to press on with courage because I was now solidly anchored in my faith and *could not* be moved.

CHAPTER SEVENTEEN

THE MIRACLE OF REPENTANCE

"And though the Lord give you the bread of adversity, and the water of affliction, yet shall not thy teachers be removed into a corner any more, but thine eyes shall see thy teachers: And thine ears shall hear a word behind thee, saying, This is the way, walk ye in it, when ye turn to the right hand, and when ye turn to the left." - Isaiah 30:20-21

While spending countless hours in the hospital, we soon realized we were in a school of spiritual learning and that, unbeknownst to us, we still had a few more important lessons that we needed to learn.

On Friday morning, March 7th, I was told by the doctor that if there was space available and if Lexi was doing well enough, she would be moved to the IMC Neuro Rehab Unit in Murray, Utah later that afternoon. The doctor had notified me of this possibility a few days prior, but I had doubted it would happen anytime soon, as Lexi was in such poor condition. I also felt she needed to stay in the ICU a little longer. Although I had my misgivings I also was overjoyed at the possibility of her being transferred as I knew that meant she was progressing and would be coming home sooner.

That afternoon, the head of the clinic at IMC met with me and said Lexi qualified to go. Within a few minutes, we were packing up her few belongings, and she was loaded onto a gurney and taken in an ambulance to Murray, which is about 45 minutes away, while I followed behind in my car. After arriving at the hospital in Murray, I found that the rehabilitation unit had many benefits that the ICU did not have. For example, Lexi was not limited to the rules of the ICU and could have any amount of family with her in her room at the same time. Also, she could have friends visit her occasionally as well. Another benefit was that Lexi had a CNA assigned to be with her at all times to ensure she would never be alone. This meant we did not have to worry about having a family member with her at night. The following day, Saturday morning, the rehab staff started physical therapy with Lexi. My girls had offered to go to the hospital, so I could spend time with my grandchildren before they had to return to their homes out of state. It was all I could do to not go to the hospital, and by 9:00 a.m., I knew I could not stay away from Lexi any longer and left the kids with my son Parker.

Just as I walked into the rehab gym, I saw Lexi grab hold of two railings on either side of her and pull herself out of her wheel chair to a standing position. But as she did so, she cried out in excruciating pain and sat back down. Very concerned, I ran across the room to see what was wrong. However the physical therapist explained that her brain signals were not working correctly, which meant that she thought she was in pain when she really wasn't. They further explained that her response was a completely normal reaction for a person with a traumatic brain injury.

I told them that I didn't believe that it was her brain playing tricks on her but that she was truly in pain. But because I didn't accept their theory, they went on to ask me if I'd read the information booklet discussing brain injuries. When I informed them that I had not read it, they told me it was essential that I did and one of the therapists immediately left to get me a copy. When he returned, I took the book but didn't read it because I knew the pain she was experiencing was real and was not a result of her brain injury.

I allowed them to have Lexi try to stand one more time. Again she cried out in agony and sat back down. At this point in her recovery, Lexi was not able to speak much so she wasn't able to describe the intensity of the pain or where it was coming from, yet the sound of her scream and the terrified grimace on her face said it all. I shuddered to see her in so much pain and was upset that I had allowed them to have her stand again.

I told the therapists that she wouldn't scream--especially with such intensity - unless she was experiencing real pain. I went on to insist that her leg be X-rayed, as I felt impressed that this was where the pain was stemming from. I also knew Lexi's unconquerable spirit and that if she wasn't in pain, she would be doing all she could to learn to stand again. I felt God guiding my steps as it was "given [to me] by the Comforter what [I should] do" (D&C 31:11).

> *"He only is my rock and my salvation: he is my defense; I shall not be moved."*
> *- Psalms 62:6*

Before they took her for the exam, they tried to talk me out of it again, reminding me it was Saturday and, as such, I was inconveniencing a lot of people needlessly. They were certain it would be a waste of the doctor's time and my resources, but I wouldn't back down. Although annoyed at my demands, they granted me my request, and Lexi was taken down to the radiology department for an X-ray.

When the results of the X-ray came back, they verified that Lexi had indeed suffered an injury to her leg. She had fractured her tibia, likely by hitting the side of the car during the accident. The exam also revealed that her tibia was split completely in half, thus explaining why she was screaming in so much distress.

Later that day, the physician came to Lexi's room to explain the two options he had for fixing her leg. The first option included placing a thigh-high hard cast onto her leg that she would need to wear for eight weeks. The second choice included doing surgery to place a metal rod in her leg. Doing surgery would mean that she could be up and walking on her leg soon after the operation. If she had the hard cast she would not be able to walk on it for eight weeks.

After explaining these options, the doctor stated he was certain surgery would be the best solution. I was worried for her to go into surgery because she still required oxygen, and I was afraid she would have to be intubated again and put back into the ICU after the operation. I was also worried that she wouldn't wake up from the procedure. However the doctor explained that Lexi wouldn't have to be put under anesthesia as she would be given a spinal block for the surgery that would allow her to be awake during the procedure. After considering the possibilities and learning that the doctor was confident that surgery was the way to go, I followed his advice and we agreed to schedule it for the following morning.

Upon arriving back at the hospital for the surgery in the darkness of chilly early morning air, Doug and I were told it would take about an hour and then we would be able to see Lexi in recovery. However, after two hours had gone by with no word about how she was, I found myself starting to get concerned. After we had waited for almost three hours, we finally got a call from the surgeon telling us that the surgery had gone well and that the rod had been placed in her leg.

Following that phone call, the anesthesiologist came to inform us that although the plan was to do a spinal block for her surgery, he had been unable to get the needle into her spine. As a result, he had to put her under anesthesia and she still had not woken up. The look on his face told me what I already knew deep down inside.

After hearing this, I was devastated! Lexi being put-under had been my fear about doing the surgery from the beginning, as I knew her lungs hadn't fully recovered from the accident. But despite my foreboding fears, all we could do was wait. I paced impatiently back and forth in the waiting room, endless questions marching through my mind. Each minute that passed chipped away at my peace. I took a calming breathe and braced myself for the bad news, as I picked up the phone and called the operating room to see if we could finally go back and see her.

There was a moment of silence on the other end. "Is this Lexi's mom?" a male voice asked.

"Yes. Why can't we come see Lexi?" I blurted out.

The doctor paused and then hesitantly confided to me, "She is still having a difficult time breathing and needs to be monitored."

My shoulders fell, a heaviness settled in my chest. I took a deep breath and then slowly released it feeling a growing sense of uneasiness.

"What do you mean?" My voice held a sting. "Can't we at least be in the room with her?" I asked, puzzled and distressed.

I didn't understand - even when she was in a coma, we were allowed to be with her. I knew something was amiss, just as I had known about the injury to her leg the day prior. What had gone wrong? I felt stripped of my peace once again. My buried grief returned, lodging painfully in my

> *"Who comforteth [me] in all [my] tribulation." - 2Corinthians 1:4*

heart. I struggled to regain my composure and to push my fear far from me.

"Is she....?" Doug's voice trailed off as I nodded dejectedly, reading his thoughts as he sighed with disappointment.

As the day wore on and the minutes slowly ticked by, we grew more and more anxious to see her. Although I was extremely frustrated, I tried to "be patient in [this affliction]" and to endure, in order to have God with me (D&C 24:8). But no answers were forthcoming.

After all she'd been through, I wondered how this could be happening. Yet somehow I knew deep down it was our family's fault she was not doing well. This is because there had been some fault finding on that Friday and Saturday before the surgery which had gravely bothered me. A few of our family members had become mildly upset after briefly debating on the  number of visitors that should be allowed to visit Lexi as well as whether their children were being watched over properly while they were at the hospital. I believe our family's conflict had negatively affected Lexi, similar to when Joseph Smith was not able to translate after having words with Emma until he prayed for forgiveness. (David Whitmer "Address to All Believers in Christ" March 19, 1881. B.H. Roberts, "Defense of the Faith and the Saints", Vol.1)

Besides the disunity, I also knew that our prayers weren't as intense as they had been at the beginning and had become more casual as she started to improve. When the accident first happened, we had stretched our very beings by living a higher level of obedience and spirituality than we had ever before. Somehow we had let ourselves become lax and drift to a lower level of commitment as she progressed. At this time, the Spirit whispered to me that because the Lord had been the one to save Lexi, He could still take her back at any time if we did not always remember our complete dependence on Him. In other words, God would "prove [us] whether [we would] keep the way of the Lord to walk therein...or not" (Judges 2:22).

> *"For verily, verily, I say unto you, he that hath the spirit of contention is not of me, but is of the devil, who is the father of contention, and he stirreth up the hearts of men to contend with anger, one with another." - 3 Nephi 11:29*

I started to plead to the Lord for forgiveness. I was sorry for not living up to what He expected of me and for anything I had done that might have caused her to return to the ICU. In my prayer I "entered into a covenant to seek the Lord God...with *all* [my] heart and with *all* [my] soul" (2 Chronicles 15:12, emphasis added). I prayed to hear what I needed to hear and to do what I needed to do.

Finally, after the many hours of waiting, I heard the doctor call my name and I whirled around to face the inevitable. He informed us that Lexi had been admitted to the Neuro Shock ICU where she had been intubated again. And due to the surgery and pneumonia, she was struggling to breathe on her own. They had put on very high ventilator settings (70% oxygen), which was the most breathing assistance she had ever needed.

The doctors did just about every test possible to find out what the problem was and why she was struggling to breathe. They assumed that it was a pulmonary embolism which is when a blood clot blocks one or more of the arteries to her lungs, obstructing her airway. Yet the tests didn't show that as being the reason why she was not able to breathe on her own.

It was horrible and very disappointing to see Lexi unconscious and back at the ICU, yet I knew without a doubt that God was in charge of her future. If we wanted Heavenly Father to continue to be with Lexi, then we would have to show it not only through our faith but also through our works.

That evening my son Tanner came to the hospital and offered to give her another priesthood blessing. As Tanner started to give the blessing, he paused mid-sentence and couldn't go on. As I listened to him struggle for words, my heart sank. A deafening silence descended upon the room. I knew how spiritually in tune Tanner was and how powerful his past blessings had been, and my heart clutched with fear. I realized that what I had felt throughout the day was coming true--that Lexi might not be healed. As Tanner continued to pause,

"Hast thou not procured this unto thyself, in that thou hast forsaken the Lord thy God, when he led thee by the way"? (Jeremiah 2:17)

I began to pray with greater fervency for our Father in Heaven to heal her, and I pondered if the Lord would allow Lexi to continue to be with us. I chided myself for anything I might have said or

> *"And in nothing doth man offend God...save those who confess not His hand in all things..."*
> *- D&C 59:21*

done to cause the rift between us and God's healing power to Lexi. Finally, after what seemed like an eternity, the words came to Tanner, and he was able to finish the blessing. I breathed an audible sigh of relief.

Afterwards he told us that he was being rebuked by the Lord for our entire family. He explained that we had been too lax in our pleadings on behalf of Lexi to the Lord. We had just *expected* the miracle to continue on, without being grateful to Him and acknowledging *His* hand in it all.

I had not said anything to Tanner about my concerns before the blessing, yet the Spirit told us both individually that Heavenly Father was not pleased with us for forgetting to rely on Him more fully during Lexi's recovery. Lowering my voice to a whisper, I told Tanner that I had known all day that the Lord was not happy with our family for not being exactly obedient and that it was the cause for the delay in Lexi's progress. We had not been fixed on God's purpose in order to have the heavens opened to us. I knew from the very beginning of her accident that we couldn't engage in conflict because of the enormous price we would pay in driving the Spirit away, as well as the angels that were attending to her. We prayed for forgiveness and committed to do better. And soon a radiance welled up inside me, and I knew we had been forgiven.

Although we felt an immeasurable sense of reprieve that Lexi had once again been spared, we were weary and spent. Thankfully, our friends were at the hospital visiting a mutual friend when his wife felt impressed that both Doug and I might be in need of blessings. They called up to our room before they left to offer us that gift. Sometimes the realities of life seemed harsh, but gratefully the benevolence of loved ones dissolved those feelings and opened my eyes to see more clearly the good in the world.

By the time we headed home, the air outside had turned cool, and dusk had already settled over the city. The once busy streets were now seemingly empty when we got into our car. Although I was sad because of another setback, relief surged through me knowing each step of the way we had been blessed with sensitive hearts and inspired minds to give us what we needed. We would "hope continually" (Psalms 71:14). We would "go in the strength of the Lord" so that the Lord would "incline [His] ear unto [us]" (Psalms 71:16, 1).

Because of the trials Lexi had just gone through and the fact that she was back in ICU again, my daughter Shelby suggested that we start a continuous fast for her. Each day of the week, a member of our family would fast so that every day someone would be fasting for her. Individually we felt that we needed to show the Lord we were serious about our commitment in calling down His power from heaven to heal Lexi both mentally and physically. Through every setback, trial, and heartache our family experienced, we were able to say with absolute clarity, "My God hath been my support...He hath filled me with his love...he hath heard my cry by day, and he hath given me knowledge by visions in the nighttime...O Lord, I will praise thee forever; yea my soul will rejoice in thee, my God, and the rock of my salvation" (2 Nephi 4:20-21, 23, 30).

God did indeed hear our prayers of repentance and thanksgiving because the next day Lexi was extubated, although she continued to need the ventilator. We had learned a very valuable lesson that would stay with us the rest of our lives as we uncovered what God was trying to teach us. It was a clear reminder that our actions do indeed determine how much the powers of Heaven can be distilled upon us and our loved ones. The earlier pain and darkness I had experienced transformed into joy and into light. It flowed through me and penetrated my heart.

CHAPTER EIGHTEEN

THE MIRACLE OF THE WHISPERINGS OF THE SPIRIT

"Hast thou not known? Hast thou not heard, that the everlasting God, the Lord, the Creator of the ends of the earth, fainteth not, neither is weary? there is no searching of his understanding." - Isaiah 40:28

On the first day we arrived at the rehab center - before we had discovered her broken leg - the doctor asked Lexi who I was in order to asses her memory. Up to this point in her recovery, she had always answered that question correctly. But on this day, she looked at me and said, without hesitation in a voice slightly slurred and lifeless, "Michael Jackson."

My eyes widened and a chill shot through me. The doctor then pointed to my daughter Shelby and asked who she was, and Lexi said feebly, "A rock star," her face expressionless.

With a look of horror, I glanced at my daughter Shelby. From the moment Lexi had come out of the coma, her brain and memory had seemed to be intact, so I couldn't understand why she would answer this way now. At first, I thought she might have been teasing us with her comical answers and waited for her to giggle, but she didn't.

The rehab doctor informed us that her bizarre answers were totally normal for someone with a brain injury. But to me, her answers were very worrisome. However, I knew things would be ok in the long run because of the priesthood blessings she had been given that said she'd make a full recovery, so I brushed aside my concern.

I didn't have much time to think about her odd

"but the spirit iself maketh intercession for us." - Rom.8:26.

behavior, because the very next day was the day we learned that her tibia had been broken which resulted in her returning to the ICU. All our thoughts and prayers were then focused on her regaining the ability to breathe on her own again. But a few days after she was stabilized in the ICU, Lexi was muttering some phrases that didn't make sense. My heart was troubled. This time the Spirit whispered to me that it wasn't her head injury that was causing her to say these outlandish comments. I immediately jumped up from my chair to find a nurse and asked her to check the medications that Lexi was on and what the side effects were. Sure enough, one of the side effects of her medications caused hallucinations. I told the nurse to take her off that drug immediately.

Almost daily I felt guided by God in Lexi's behalf, as thoughts would come into my mind's eye to know how to help Lexi. I can attribute this in a large part to a blessing my son-in-law Daniel had given me a few days after the accident where he promised me that in every instance, I would be inspired and prompted to know exactly what to do to facilitate Lexi's healing. In every way and through every experience, I could see that the blessing he gave me was being fulfilled: "it [was] given [me] in the very moment what [I] should speak" and do (D&C 24:6) for "the still small voice...pierceth all things" (D&C 85:6). I was relying on inspiration, not knowledge, and that made all the difference.

When Lexi's doctor came to check up on her, I asked him why he had been giving that particular drug to Lexi. He told me that he was just continuing to administer the same medicine the doctors from the previous hospital had prescribed for her. He continued to explain to me that those pills were usually given to treat Alzheimer patients but that occasionally some doctors used them for patients with severe brain injuries to help their memory.

I was not happy when I heard this since her mind had been good from the moment she awoke from her coma. I felt they were using Lexi as a guinea pig and that the medicine was making her thought patterns worse. It came as a great relief to have the doctor agree with me and to be willing to back me up by writing on her chart that she was allergic to that particular drug so she would not be given it again.

It took a week or more for that medication to wear off. In the meantime, her conversations continued to be a little odd. She alternated regularly between fantasy and reality. One of the side effects of the medicine caused her to be obsessed with the piano. Everything she mentioned had the word piano in it. She would say with considerable anxiety on her face, "I want to wear my pajama pants. They are over there in my piano drawer," or "I can't go for a walk because I need to practice the piano." Disappointment crossed her face when I told her the hospital didn't have a piano.

One afternoon she begged me to let her have the phone to text her friends to thank them for a sweet note they'd written her, but instead of thanking them for the letter, she thanked them for their beautiful piano concerto. Still another day, her eyes shining with hope, she muttered, "Is that popcorn over there?" pointing towards the sink in her room.

I looked at her without even a small hint of amusement, "Nope." A shiver ran through me when I thought of her nonsensical talk.

> *"Let a double portion of thy spirit be upon me."*
> *- 2 Kgs. 2:9.*

The Miracle of the Whisperings of the Spirit

"Are you sure?" Her voice was soft. She let out a sigh, her shoulders slumped slightly. She was determined there was popcorn everywhere and wanted some desperately.

Other times she seemed distraught and puzzled when we would try to get her to do therapy, believing instead that she should be at school.

"I'm late, I have a class right now," she would say obviously agitated. "I... I'm going to fail my classes, so I can't do therapy." She seemed stressed and worried.

I felt more than just a twinge of concern and swallowed my nervousness. I would remind her that she was in the hospital because she had been hit by a car and that her teachers knew about the accident, so she didn't need to worry. Luckily my words usually sufficed, and she would settle her thoughts back to what was happening around her.

One morning, like every other morning, I walked in and kissed her on the cheek. She would usually smile when I would do this, but on this particular day because of the medicine she was on, she scowled at me and growled, "Why do you keep doing that?" Her voice still low and reserved.

"Because I love you" I responded.

"Well it's not fair"

"What's not fair?"

"I can't love you back!" she mumbled in quiet frustration. I suppressed a smile at her innocent response. Even though she was confused, she still felt guilty that she was a taker and not a giver.

On other occasions, she would forget family member's names even though she had known their name from the beginning of her recovery. One day, my daughter Kelsi came to visit Lexi on her lunch break. Testing Lexi's memory, I pointed to Kelsi when she walked in the room and asked, "What's her name?"

Lexi looked at her with a blank stare. "I don't remember," her voice strained in a whisper. Her shoulders lifted then fell in disappointment.

I was surprised that she couldn't remember, so in order to help jog her memory I asked her questions about our home.

"Do you remember that we have chickens at home?"

She responded in the affirmative. "What are their names?" I asked.

Without hesitation she said, "Daisy, Ace and Dixie."

My daughter Kelsi immediately blurted out, "You remember the chicken's names, but you don't remember my name?"

Thinking that she would remember her sister's name now I pointed to Kelsi again and asked, "So what's her name?"

She gave Kelsi a quizzical look and then as if suddenly remembering she blurted out, "Daisy?" (the name of our chicken). I struggled to maintain a straight face.

Lexi's face twisted into a knitted brow. "I know who you are. I just can't think of your name right now." Her voice trailed off in regret. It was frustrating for her not to remember.

The very next day my son Tanner came to visit Lexi. He often made the 45-minute trip on TRAX, the commuter train, by himself or with his wife Mandy to visit Lexi. He had taken a lot of time away from his schooling at the beginning of the accident and he was worried he would not pass his classes at BYU. But Lexi was his first priority, and he continued to make the trips to be with her, giving up much needed sleep to do so.

When visitors entered Lexi's room, as a normal routine, the nurses would quiz Lexi to facilitate her memory, and today was no exception. "Who is this guy?" the nurse asked.

Lexi blurted out without the smallest hint of a grin, "My boyfriend."

Tanner and I stood there in stunned silence. Was her memory that bad? But quick as a wink, she grinned sheepishly, "Just kidding. He's my brother."

Tanner tipped back his head and laughed hysterically. Unbeknownst to us, for the past few days Lexi had been listening to our concerns about her memory and decided to play a trick on us. I was relieved and laughed for days about how she had managed to tease us. She had given us a needed distraction from the mundane hospital life. And it was also a good indication of how sharp her mind was to come up with that joke on her own and to do it in the spur of the moment.

When Lexi could start comprehending things more clearly towards the end of the week, I asked her, "Do you remember how you had talked about being a motivational speaker for the last couple of years?"

Lexi had decided in high school that she wanted to be a motivational speaker and would talk to me quite often about her career choice. Speaking in public wasn't easy for her, but she was determined to become a polished orator. She was excited for her first public speaking class at BYU, and with that in mind, it came as a big surprise when she walked in the door one weekend and exclaimed, "Mom, I need a new major!"

I stopped what I was doing and turned around to face her. "What?...Why is that?" I inquired. She was not one to just change majors on a whim. When she had a goal, she stuck with it. I was perplexed by her statement.

"Yeah.... I can't be a motivational speaker anymore," she said.

"Why would you say that? I asked, genuinely surprised.

"So...it just dawned on me that every motivational speaker has a bad accident," she said shrugging her shoulders. "So yeah, can't be one now." Her smile had long since faded and the sparkle had left her eyes. She had convinced herself that her long-held dream was no longer a possibility.

Remembering our previous conversation, Lexi now rolled her eyes and shook her head as if to say, "Oh man, I really jinxed myself didn't I?"

> *"And I was led by the spirit not knowing beforehand the things which I should do."*
> *- 1 Nephi 4:6.*

God did have a plan for Lexi as he does for each of us, but it was exhilarating to have a front row seat and see the events of her life unfold. I couldn't help but marvel, especially when I reflected on how through the whisperings of the Spirit the Lord was able to direct me to know the best way to help her recover.

CHAPTER NINETEEN

THE MIRACLE OF BEING PATIENT

"...that ye live in thanksgiving daily, for the many mercies and blessings which he doth bestow upon you." - Alma 34:38

We were extremely excited the following Wednesday when Lexi was allowed to leave the ICU - for the second time - and go back upstairs to the rehab center. When she left, they gave her a small respiratory mask that formed a mist. When inhaled, it helped her with her breathing difficulties--which is what I was concerned about. However, much to our dismay, within a couple hours, she was back down in the ICU again.

My husband, Doug, had arrived late in the evening to be with Lexi until she fell asleep for the night, so I left to go home. Before I left, I gave strict instructions to both him and the nurse that Lexi was not to have more medicine than the dosage she was allotted. I repeated these instructions several times. For some reason, I was worried she would be given too much.

He was a little annoyed with me for my repeated

instructions, thinking I didn't trust him, but I just felt a foreboding about her receiving too much medication that night and almost didn't leave the hospital because of it. Within a half hour after I left, the nurse gave Lexi her medication. About that time, Lexi had some visitors that stayed for about ten minutes or so.

After they left, he and the nurse were sitting with Lexi, when the nurse got a startled look on her face and asked, "Does Lexi look grey to you?"

Doug jumped up and tried to wake Lexi. She was unresponsive. He shook her arms and nudged her, trying to wake her up, but she didn't respond. He started to panic and yelled at the nurse to get someone right away. Within what seemed like a minute there were 15 people in her room (code red over the intercom really brings hospital staff from everywhere!) working frantically to revive her.

Soon after, he called me to tell me what was happening. I shot up from my chair, my tired limbs completely forgotten for the news of Lexi. My mind was racing, my stomach tightened in fear, "What happened? Is she alright?" My words chocked in my throat." Is she breathing?" My heart was thumping wildly in my chest searching for answers. I didn't want to submit "to all things which the Lord [saw] fit to inflict" upon me (Mosiah 3:19). I was drowning in grief, hardly believing that this could be occurring again when less than an hour before she had been happy and talking. In the back of my

mind I wondered how I could possibly survive another heart-wrenching ordeal. Tears spilled down my cheeks, my knees gave way and I collapsed on the floor. I couldn't wrap my mind around what had just happened.

My daughter Cassidy, seeing my condition, went next door to ask our neighbor, who is also her father-in-law, if he would come give me a blessing. As he placed his hands on my head, my crying subsided and my eyes no longer burned. I felt a strong feeling of confirmation come over me, and I knew she would be okay as the import of his words sunk deep. The Savior was there again for me to heal my "wounded soul" (Jacob 2:8). I was learning first-hand how He was indeed sent to "heal the brokenhearted" (Luke 4:18). And this time I was reassured her condition had nothing to do with our family's

righteousness.

Sensing how devastated I was, Doug called back and told me I didn't need to return to the hospital because Lexi had stabilized and everything was

> *"Life has peaks and shadows ....The Lord in His wisdom does not shield anyone from grief or sadness...so how can we love days that are filled with sorrow? We can't—at least not in the moment. . But, the way we react to adversity can be a major factor in how happy and successful we can be" - Joseph B. Wirthlin, "Come What May, and Love It," Ensign, Nov. 2008*

fine. He didn't let me know that she still hadn't regained consciousness. However, our friends, who were just leaving the hospital when Lexi stopped breathing, heard the code red signal over the intercom. They knew Lexi's room number and stopped to ask someone what the code red meant. Upon hearing the severity of the situation, they called our friend who came to the hospital and stayed until Lexi regained consciousness, for which we were immensely grateful for. The doctors were worried that Lexi would slip back into a coma and suffer additional brain damage from the lack of oxygen.

We learned several days later that the pharmacist had written a prescription for three times the amount of medication that Lexi was supposed to be given, which is why she had stopped breathing. We were grateful that the Spirit let us know immediately that this setback was not because of something we had done or failed to do. But it was a reminder to me that even though we might be doing our very best to pray and focus on the Savior, bad things still happen.

It was terrifying to think how close we came to losing Lexi that night. The Lord may have wept seeing us in such turmoil of spirit as He does for all those who suffer similar trials. The scriptures teach us about this aspect of the Savior's divine nature: "And it came to pass that the God of heaven looked upon the residue of the people, and he wept" (Moses 7:28). As Jeffrey R. Holland has said, "He does hear us. He does see us. He does love us....And

> "...we glory in tribulations also: knowing that tribulation worketh patience: And patience, experience: and experience, hope:"
> - Rom. 5:3-4

when we weep He and the angels of heaven weep with us" ("Lessons from Liberty Jail," CES Devotional, September 2008).

Although we were extremely grateful that Lexi was alive, we were discouraged that she had to be intubated again, as this set her back quite a few steps in her recovery. The Apostle Paul's words couldn't have been more poignant to us that we had "need of patience...after [we had] done the will of God" (Hebrews 10:36). As we waited for Lexi's body to heal, we were being taught that "tribulation worketh patience" (Romans 5:3). I was allowed to internalize the omnipotence of the Savior more completely through this type of suffering. As described in Isaiah, "For a small moment [I felt] forsaken...but with everlasting kindness [I was given] mercy" (Isaiah 54:7-8). I continued to experience for myself that coming to Christ and allowing Him to carry my load was the only way to peace.

CHAPTER TWENTY

THE MIRACLE OF BEING FILLED
WITH LIGHT

"...and the sheep follow him: for they know his voice." - John 10:4

At 5:00 a.m. the next morning, I returned to the hospital, determined that there would not be another setback in Lexi's recovery. I was devastated that she was back in the ICU unit--intubated and hooked up with a catheter--for the third time. It seemed that each time she began to make a small amount of progress, something unforeseen would happen, resulting in her having to regain her faculties over again. But I needed to remember the command, "Be strong and of a good courage" (Deuteronomy 31:6).

It was around 7:00 a.m. when Lexi's trauma doctor made his rounds to her room. Having been informed of my concerns and knowing this was our third time in the ICU, he was genuinely sympathetic and invited me to write a list of issues that I felt needed to be addressed. He said they would distribute it to the staff to use as a guideline. His invitation startled me, and I was touched to see the understanding in his eyes. It was refreshing to have a doctor of his prestige, who was humble enough to ask for my opinion and suggestions and then to follow them, instead of insisting that because of his superior knowledge with trauma patients, he should be the sole expert. His face was kind and gentle. Each day he had me brief him on what I felt her needs were and how I thought they could best help her. In just a few short days, he taught me about compassion, humility, and the gift of listening. The head nurse also went the extra mile, giving me her personal phone number to call when she was not at the hospital. I was touched by their genuine interest in Lexi's well-being.

One request I made was for Lexi be given more time

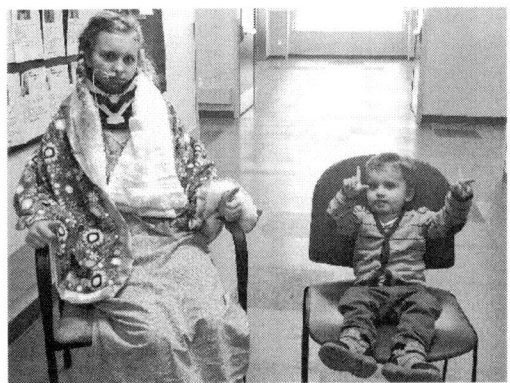 with her therapist. They quickly obliged, starting Lexi on the long process of learning to walk again. She had two physical therapists take her a few hundred yards down the hall and back, her oxygen tank in tow, as she inched forward down the hall. Sometimes she couldn't make it down the hall, and they would

grab a chair for her until she gained enough strength to return to the room.

When we went on these exceedingly short walks, I found it amusing that she would immediately head to the drinking fountain. It was always a huge disappointment to her when she was told she couldn't have any water. Eventually she was allowed to get a small, one-inch sponge attached to a stick to dip in water. The joy she expressed in getting a few drops of water is etched in my memory, and it will always make me happy to think of it. As she dipped the sponge in the water, she would beam and exclaim,

> "...men are, that they might have joy." - 2 Nephi

"YUMMMY!" A tiny smile would light up her eyes. Each time she tasted the water, she would say the same thing over and over, with as much fervor and joy as she could muster. Her face was a picture of pure delight.

She was still enjoying her drops of water the second day after she returned to the ICU when her two-year-old nephew Calvin came to visit. He observed her delight as she squeezed the water out of the sponge into her mouth. Of course seeing her enjoyment, he wanted what she was having. So I got a cup of water and sponge for him and sat him in the bed next to her. I thought for sure he would be disappointed when he tasted it and found out it was just water. Much to our surprise, he was just as thrilled as Lexi. They would both squeal in delight chanting, "Yummy! Yummy!" and look at each other and giggle. It was as if they had just raided the candy store and were relishing their tasty morsels. A smile stole across my face feeling their joy. Moments like this, when we could laugh, helped ease our burden. We found humor was a gift and we cherished any time we could laugh and enjoy playful encounters with one another.

After a few days Lexi was strong enough to leave the ICU and return to the rehab floor. I was wary of her going back since the previous two times she had returned to the rehab center, it had taken less than a day to get readmitted to the ICU. Luckily for Lexi, her progress went uphill from that moment on, with only a few minor complications.

Early in the morning on her second day back in the rehab center, I was standing talking to Lexi's doctor when I heard Lexi weakly mutter, "Thanks". Out of the corner of my eye I saw that a technician who had come to check the equipment in the room was just leaving and Lexi was acknowledging him for his service. A few minutes later as I continued my discussion with the doctor, a cleaning lady came in the room and took out the garbage. Again I heard a barely audible "thank you" from Lexi. Since her room was always a revolving door of visitors, it wasn't long before a nurse

appeared in the room to check her vitals, and once again there
was a raspy, unclear "thanks" coming from her lips.

This time I stopped talking and turned to look over at
Lexi. I was dumbfounded. Here she was lying in a hospital bed
with a neck brace that made it virtually impossible to move her

> *"It might sound contrary to the wisdom of the world to suggest that one who is burdened with sorrow should give thanks to God. But those who set aside the bottle of bitterness and lift instead the goblet of gratitude can find a purifying drink of healing, peace, and understanding." - Dieter F. Uchtdorf, "Grateful in Any Circumstances," Ensign, May 2014*

head. I also knew how sore and tender her throat was from
having the breathing tube taken in and out over the last several
weeks. Plus she had a feeding tube in her nose and her head
hurt so much that she would cry out in agony every few hours,
begging for more pain medication to ease the pounding in her
head. She wouldn't even allow me to touch her hair and would
scream if I did because of how tender her scalp was. Yet here
she was showing gratitude to people right and left as they came
into her room to perform their normal everyday duties.

I continued to observe her the rest of the day and
noticed that she never stopped showing her appreciation, even
when they asked her to do something she detested, like making
her blow puffs of air into her oxygen device. She was always
sincere, her eyes shining with goodness. I had to chuckle under

my breath when the nurse came back with a syringe and slid the needle into her forearm. With teeth clenched, Lexi still managed to whisper a quiet "thank you" as she grimaced in discomfort.

I think I heard her say thank you at least 30 times a day.

> *"Christ shall give thee light." - Eph. 5:14.*

She had every excuse not to be thankful and to resent the fact she couldn't eat, walk, or swallow, yet she had a spirit of gratitude. I knew I needed to save what I had just experienced to that portion of my brain for safe keeping. I wanted this mental picture indelibly etched in my mind.

I lay down next to her, putting my legs inside her blankets and gently took her hand as I laid my head on her shoulder and closed my eyes. I just wanted to be next to her, hoping that maybe some of her goodness would seep deep into my soul and change me for the better. She was so good and Christlike. The evening shadows began to emerge, darkening her room, and stillness permeated our space. Although I could still hear the humming of the machines surrounding her bed, the place seemed suddenly still and peaceful. As I continued to nestle next to her, my heart swelled with thanksgiving for each and every day that she had been allowed to remain with us. Oh how I loved her! Throughout her life she had taught me by her example, and now she was teaching me again that true character is manifested by how we react when faced with adversity. As I had watched her throughout the day, I understood more completely how gratitude does indeed have the power to bring us happiness in the worst of circumstances.

Each day I seemed to glean something from Lexi, and the next afternoon proved to be no exception. She asked me in her still faint voice, "Can you tell me some stories that happened to me in the hospital? Because I have no memory of anything."

"Hmmm, let's see..." my voice trailed off, as I tried to think of a story I had not told her.

"Remember when she started kicking her leg after being so still? Tanner said with a sly grin on his face.

I started to laugh as I rested my hand lightly on her arm. "Oh yeah...you were still in a coma, but you started kicking your left leg up and down over and over again until you were almost off the bed. Mandy was standing at the foot of your bed at the time and gently moved your legs away from the side of the bed and tucked them under your sheet."

"That's nice of her," Lexi chimed in.

"Yes it was nice of her because you were getting really close to the edge of the bed with that kicking motion. But just as she got your feet situated...you picked up your leg again and...kicked her in the stomach.

"Yeah," Tanner snickered, "I had been watching this unfold across the room and I was thinking to myself, 'Holy cow, she is one determined girl. She's letting us know even in a coma, to not mess with her.' It was hilarious, Lex, we couldn't stop laughing."

Lexi's reaction to the story was priceless. She bemoaned, "Why would I do that?!.....Did I tell her I was sorry?"

I tried hard not to smile at her sweet, innocent response and leaned down to stroke her hair. I caught her eye and winked at her, "No, Lexi, you were in a coma....but that is so kind of you to care about her feelings. I'm sure she understood."

Lexi perfectly fit the description "the Lord thy God is with thee whithersoever thou goest" (Joshua 1:9). She was truly filled with light.

CHAPTER TWENTY- ONE

THE MIRACLE OF FACING TOWARD THE SON

"...know thou, my son, that all these things shall give thee experience, and shall be for thy good. The Son of Man hath descended below them all. Art thou greater than he?" - D&C 122:7-8

On the night of her accident, three of Lexi's good friends wanted to do something for her. They decided to set up a page on Facebook called "Pray for Lexi." It was a brilliant idea. The page was shared by hundreds of people from all over the world. It soon garnered well over 32,000 followers in less than a week, as the news converged on the Internet, with some posts exceeding 300,000 views.

It was a great blessing to Lexi to have so many people praying and fasting for her. Our family took over managing the page the day after the accident, because it was the fastest and most convenient way to give updates on her condition. My daughter Kelsi wrote each post from the information I provided her for the first two weeks, and then I took over managing it completely until Lexi was able to do so herself several months later. It's clear that Lexi's friends were inspired to set up this page after reading how Lexi's story affected so many people for good.

A common thread came from those we had never met but prayed for her nonetheless: "I don't know you or your family, but I want you to know your story has touched my life. I fasted for Lexi and your family today. Miracles happen!"

Another poster wrote, "This is so beautiful. I will keep praying for this darling girl who I don't even know and have never met. I know all these prayers from all these wonderful people are helping this sweet girl. God is a God of miracles! We have all witnessed one with your post today. Thank you for sharing…Heaven's help was near."

We also received a message from a lady who told us that as she was shopping on Saturday, the day before the fast, the sweetest little girl handed her a flyer with Lexi's story and the title "Pray For Lexi" on it. Our neighbor Todd had created and distributed thousands of these flyers, with the help of neighbors, to get the word out. She thought it was touching and wrote, "Of course I have kept her in my prayers. That little girl who handed the flyer to me was so precious. I thought how important it is for each of us to 'bear one another's burdens.'"

We were so grateful for these acts of kindness and compassion. And not only was Lexi blessed because of those who fasted and prayed for her, but there were countless others whose hearts were softened and inspired to believe in God again. For example, this was a note that came to my daughter:

"Hi Kelsi, It's [name removed] from high school. I am sure you have had many messages come through about your sister. But I felt like I really needed to tell you--and maybe your sister one day - how deeply touched I am by her story. I've also read your sister-in-law's blog post (Mandy) and I have been following "Pray for Lexi"!

Anyways, I have been struggling with the gospel and the Church since September of last year, give or take. It hasn't been easy, and at times I wonder why I am wasting my time. Recently, the past month about, I have been praying to understand why I feel the way I do. I was raised in a great LDS home, my husband has a strong testimony of the Church, but he wasn't going to push something on me...he wanted me to figure it out on my own. I was invited to follow "Pray for Lexi" and reading the posts, and seeing the faith your sweet family has, and the love you have for the gospel has truly touched me. I owe it to Lexi and your family for helping me realize what was right and what I needed in my life. Thank you! Thank you! Thank you! You and your family are so amazing! I will keep you in my prayers."

And there are even more examples of the dramatic change that was occurring in the lives of many:

"I know my prayer for her last night was the first time I have prayed in months."

Mona explained, "You have touched me in so many ways and helped restore my faith in God just when I thought I'd lost it forever. You are a living angel. Bless you."

Becky wrote from far-away Africa of their new-found understanding of prayer: "The Bible says, "If Christ be for us, who can be against us?' Lexi, my friends and I in Ghana are praying for you and I know it's just a matter of time, you will be up on your feet again. You're a very strong girl and nothing can break you down, not even what the doctor says…you're not just a fighter, you're a VICTOR. Your story has challenged me for the fact that, no mountain is too high to prevent God's divine miracle from reaching us. Christ is bigger than whatever you're going through. You don't know how much strength people from all the ends of the world are pulling from your story. You're rising up again to be what you've always dreamed of becoming. Lots of love from Ghana, and, LEX, nothing is impossible for our CHRIST."

And a young 19-year-old named Braxton serving a mission for our church drew strength from the prayers for Lexi as well. He felt inspired to use her story in teaching the power of prayer. Braxton wrote:

"So last Monday I felt pretty low, I wasn't too happy because I was thinking about what happened to Lexi Hansen. We had our P-day[21] as normal and went out to work at night. We had a lesson with a lady who is 27 and less active, almost inactive, and her son who is 14. Well she had a thing on her fridge that talked about praying as a family. So the thought came to me to talk to her about prayer. As we shared a scriptures, Lexi's story came to mind. As I shared the story of what had happened and how she had improved through the faith and prayer of so many faithful saints, the story brought the Spirit into the room and you could feel its presence. She felt it and by the end was completely speechless as the Spirit testified to her of the power of prayer. Ever since then, she has been praying morning and night and attended church for the second time in my five months here."

As I sat on the bed next to Lexi at the hospital, I begin to read some of these messages people had written about her on

---

[21]Preparation day. The day missionaries use to shop for food, do laundry, and prepare for the coming week.

Facebook. I wanted her to know about all the people that she had influenced through her faith and courage.

"Look at the impact you have had on so many people," I said, "They are turning to God because of you."

Lexi started to tear up and asked, perplexed, "Why?...Why would they say that?"

"Because they looked at your Facebook page to see what you had posted before the accident. A lot of these people didn't know you and wanted to see what type of person you were."

> "...who knoweth whether thou art come to the kingdom for such a time as this? - Esther 4:14

"Yeah, but what did I do? I still don't get it." Her face softened in the gentle query.

"Well... it was apparent to them from reading your posts that you had tried to *always* 'walk in the light of the Lord' (Isaiah 2:5)...that God was most important to you."

A smile touched her eyes as if she was beginning to comprehend. "What did I write about? I don't have lots of memories," she said.

"Remember...each Sunday you would write inspiring messages about God and counsel them to follow his teachings?"

She couldn't hide her emotions as her lip began to quiver, tears of joy streaming down her face, as she nestled her head on my shoulder. "Makes me so happy," she whispered reverently, a wistful smile on her face.

I knew how much this meant to her because all of her life she had wanted to turn people to Christ.

Even though Lexi had helped and was helping many people turn to Christ, one day in particular stands out in my memory—the day it was Lexi's turn to need spiritual help. It was early morning, and Lexi's occupational therapists had just come into her room to assist her to the gym where they would work with her on cognitive skills. When I tried to get Lexi out of bed, she refused to get up and started to cry and act confused and distraught over the situation. I could tell that she didn't know where she was and, even more frightening, *who* she was. She threw her arms around me and sobbed in aching despair.

I tried to console her. "Lex you are in the hospital. You had a bad accident and got hit by a car," I explained to her, but it didn't help. She continued to act irrationally. Her dark eyes clouded with uncertainty.

Suddenly I knew what to do to help her. I sprang instantly into action and ran over to a small table in the room and grabbed our family picture. In the meantime Lexi had collapsed back down on the bed, so I knelt beside the bed and pushed the picture under her face and stared intently into her eyes and asked softly, "Lexi, do you see these people? Do you know who they are?"

216

She stared intently for a long moment, her eyes moving over each family member. Almost instantly she stopped crying, her eyes softening before nodding her head "yes."

I placed my hands against her cheeks and then, releasing one hand, I pointed to her in the family picture and inquired, "Do you know who this is?"

Again there was a pause as she studied the photo. Suddenly, her eyes lit up and she slowly nodded her head "yes," a sense of recognition resting on her.

I excitedly responded, "Lexi, that's you. You are Lexi. This is your family." I could tell that her understanding of who she was and to whom she belonged had returned.

She wiped her tears with her sleeve and her lips stopped quivering as she fought for composure. I then helped her sit up in bed, and we held each other tight as now a few tears of joy escaped down her cheeks. It was a tender moment for the two of us. She knew who she was now, and a whisper of a smile

> *"Looking unto Jesus the author and finisher of our faith." - Heb. 12:2*

touched her face. She was "Lexi," a daughter of God, part of an earthly family who loved her, and that made all the difference. With that knowledge, there were no more tears and no more confusion. That message, I believe is what she had tried to portray on Facebook over the years - that we are God's children and that He loves us.

That knowledge that she was a child of God continued to burn bright as we wheeled Lexi to church services in the hospital a few days later. I don't remember anything that was said that Sunday, but I still have an image etched in my memory from that day.

The sacrament[22] had been blessed and was being passed to the congregation. Lexi, so weak and frail, instinctively reached for it, forgetting for a minute she had a feeding tube and could not swallow without aspirating. I gently held back her hand and whispered to her that although she was not able to eat the bread and drink the water, she could press it to her lips as a symbol of her desire to honor God's covenants. A forlorn look crept onto her face. For Lexi, this

---

[22] On the night before His Crucifixion, Jesus Christ met with His Apostles and instituted the sacrament (see Luke 22:19–20). Today the sacrament is an ordinance in which Church members partake of bread and water …to ponder and remember with gratitude the life, ministry, and Atonement of the Son of God.

was not enough to show her love for God; she wanted to reveal her devotion to the Lord by total and complete obedience. Lowering her head dejectedly, she stared at her clasped hands while tears tumbled gently from her eyes and onto her lap. She clearly desired to "learn...and listen...and walk in...meekness" (D&C 19:23) so that she could "always have his Spirit to be with [her]" (Moroni 4:3).

Our family members also benefited from Lexi's spiritual sensitivity. Cassidy explains:

"Lexi, in my mind, has always been so childlike. Her countenance and demeanor reflect what Christ says in the scriptures to "become as a little child" (3 Nephi 11:37). To a lot of people, Lexi may come across as naïve, but she's not. She acts according to what the Savior has taught--to be submissive and meek like unto a child. Children are very quick to forgive and forget. They are filled with an immense amount of love to all those around them. Lexi is the same. She loves everybody she meets.

When this accident happened to her, I knew right away it was because she had such an innocent and pure soul. She had important role to fulfill, and the Lord knew He could trust her to achieve a change in the lives of countless individuals throughout the world. She saw the importance of this life, grasped it firmly, and worked hard to achieve a stronger testimony and foundation of what she knew to be true. Each time I visited home after getting married, when Lexi answered the door, she did so with the biggest, brightest smile. An immediate chain reaction would take place, and I would be grinning from ear to ear. I couldn't help but think how beautiful life was. Lexi brought this spirit to everyone. She always gave me her full attention, listening to whatever I had to say and was always excited and proud of me. She had a way of bringing joy and hope to the world again.

I believe that the reason Lexi's countenance was almost always happy and filled with light is because she tried to always face towards the Son, God's Son. God reminds us to "Be of good cheer…and I will stand by you" (D&C 68:6).

Our ability to be of good cheer is in direct relation to how connected we are to Christ. Lexi stayed close to Christ and as a result could chase the darkness away when she entered a room because of the light of truth she had welcomed into her heart. Her life revealed her desire to face the Son."

THE MIRACLE OF WALKING WITH GOD

"And I will walk among you and will be your God, and ye shall be my people." - Leviticus 26:12

At this point in Lexi's recovery, my days became repetitive and routine in nature. Each morning at 5:30 a.m., I showered, dressed, in record time and went downstairs to read scriptures and say a family prayer with my son Parker, who was a senior in high school.

My husband left for work about the time I awoke. From the earliest days of our marriage, he had been an early riser and worked late into the night even on Saturdays. But with Lexi in the hospital, he gladly adjusted his schedule to stay with her during the evening hours. I was grateful for this so I could get home before Parker went to bed and to have family prayer together.

I didn't like leaving the house before Parker left for school nor did I like having him come home to an empty house, but I had no other choice. That's why the sliver of time together with him in the morning and in the evening was so important to me.After our prayer I gave Parker a hug and a kiss and hurried out the door to get to the hospital before the doctors made their rounds. More importantly, I wanted to be there before Lexi woke up

Once I got to the hospital it was actually refreshing to have a change of pace, an opportunity to have even more time to ponder, to read God's

> *"Walk in the light, as he is in the light." - 1 Jn.1:7*

word, and become better in tune with the Spirit in this sacred setting where angels had been. I sat by her window to catch the first morning rays on my open book, glancing periodically over at Lexi. I knew that I didn't want to waste time wishing for Lexi's recovery to pass but instead find out what I was to learn from this experience each day. Her challenges would refine my character as well. The more I tried to be connected to the Savior each day the happier I became.

One morning about an hour past before I heard the rustle of her sheets and some moaning. I quickly got up, took her hand and kissed it.

"Good morning, Lexi." I smiled wide, hoping to bring some sunshine to her trials.

Opening her eyes, I could tell she was tormented. "I need pills," she groaned, the words were slurred yet desperate. The suffering poured down upon her.

I swept a lock of her hair back so I could see her eyes and she instantly recoiled. I forgot again that touching her hair was off limits, including anywhere on her head. I knew instantly from seeing her pain-stricken eyes, before she had

> *"Though I walk in the midst of trouble, thou wilt revive me: thou shalt stretch forth thine hand" - Psalm 138:7*

even uttered a word, that I needed to call for a nurse to get her medicine, but the nurse was delayed.

When Lexi begged me to get the nurse again, her anguish was so intense that I could not sit idly by. The pleading in her voice pierced with force. I rushed out of the room without hesitation, searching the nurses' station and halls, but the place was deserted. Other patients were being attended to. My emotions rose to the surface, and I pursed my lips hard, swallowing back the tears to stay in control. I hated watching her suffer more than anything else. Lexi, on the other hand, couldn't hold back the tears, and they trickled down her cheeks spilling onto her pillow.

I was grateful her therapy started early because it was a good distraction from her grievous pain. I tried to help her dress, but she groaned, "I'm dressed," pointing to the basketball shorts and a t-shirt she had worn to bed. "I want to wear this," her voice trailed off.

It was obvious the throbbing in her head that lingered every minute, every second, of the day was just too much. I was sympathetic to her plight, knowing how it added to her pain and would wear her out just by changing her clothes. . Her voice exhaled in relief as she peered up at me with barely a half smile, all that she could muster.

Watching her opened my eyes to suffering I'd never seen before and that image lay heavily before me. Suffering manifested itself in her every movement. I realized there would be much more soul stretching in the slow tedious process of regaining her abilities. It was discouraging and draining at times, but I kept reminding myself that God was in charge and that His promises were real. That thought was empowering.

I put my arm around Lexi's waist and helped her out of bed. Then reaching for her hand and clutching her firmly to keep her balanced, we walked slowly and steadily a few yards to the gym. Holding her hand was the thing I cherished most about the accident. Even when she was lying in bed she'd reach over and grab it, giving me a feeling of deep satisfaction. I enjoyed these moments together. It called to my mind a much younger Lexi, her small soft hand always nestled inside of mine, clinging to me tightly where ever we went. She needed me again, needed me next to her, needed my love and encouragement. Putting my life on hold for almost a year while my life revolved around her needs changed me. It filled a longing deep inside me. I was happier. Since it was only the two of us most of the day, it bonded our relationship. We connected with a special closeness that many mothers yearn for.

She had speech, occupational, and physical therapy twice a day for half an hour each. After the three consecutive sessions, she would collapse in bed, ask for more meds and fall asleep. I didn't allow many visitors in her room, because I wanted her undisturbed in order for her to keep her strength up. However, one of her friends, Jordan, who was like family, came regularly. Most of the time, Lexi was too physically exhausted to visit, but Jordan was content just to be with her in the room.

> *"Blessed is the people that know... they shall walk, Lord, in the light of thy countenance." - Psalms 89:15.*

One late afternoon, Jordan leaned over Lexi's bed and quietly said, "I'm going to the beach tomorrow, so I won't be able to come see you for a week."

Lexi was still not talking much, so we were slightly startled to hear her whisper back pensively, "Take me with you please." Her eyes filled with disappointment. It made me misty eyed to hear her soft, but poignant, reply - and my heart sorrowed.

Jordan continued, "It will go by fast, like I'd never been gone."

And, truly, it wasn't long before we realized that, for Lexi, going to the beach might be a possibility sooner than we had hoped. She started to gain her strength back during the third week after her accident. And there was a sense of expectation that she soon would be walking by herself. Our "prayers [God had] heard, and [our] hearts [he knew]." We continually felt His "eyes [were] upon [us]." (D&C 67:1,2)

Because she had always been competitive in sports when she was younger, (probably due to having four older

brothers) it didn't surprise me to see her determination to learn to walk again. Her feisty spirit showed especially when she played basketball. It made me smile to remember some of the banter on the court when she played on the boys Junior Jazz team at 11 years old, and I became lost in my thoughts.

"Look at that... there's a girl on their team?" one of the boys on the opposing team sneered.

The boys glanced at each other smirking. Lexi glared at them with fire in her eyes and her lips drawn tight

"You'll see," one of her team mates replied defiantly.

Lexi wasn't one to venture hesitantly into a game and schooled them in the first quarter. Her team cheered and lavished Lex with praise, as a smile drifted across her face.

Her opponents' faces were pinched with panic, and they began to blame each other for their lack of scoring.

"You can't guard a girl?!" one boy snapped, giving his friend an icy stare. The smugness on their team had vanished.

"How can I lose to a girl?" another boy muttered as he stomped off the court. Lexi's athletic skill and competitive nature were always surprising to people.

Just then, the physical therapist walked in Lexi's room, pulling me away from my musings, and announced, "Are we ready for this Lexi? I think today is the day!"

Lexi had surprised everyone at the hospital by her rapid recovery and her stubborn resolve to do things faster than they thought she should. No one could have imagined on that fateful day in February that

> *"Walk in the steps of that faith of our father;" -* Rom. 4:12

she would come as far as she had, especially in such a short amount of time.

"Let's do this!" Lexi exclaimed her lips pursed together. I helped Lexi up out of bed, holding her hand we walked out of her room. Now, with a therapist on either side holding her steady, we eagerly awaited when they would allow her to walk on her own.

She continued haltingly down the main hall when one therapist said, "OK, we are going to let go of you now."

The therapists kept their hands inches from Lexi's torso in case they needed to catch her. Lexi hesitated momentarily and then began to walk on her own, cautiously placing her feet one in front of the other with great precision.

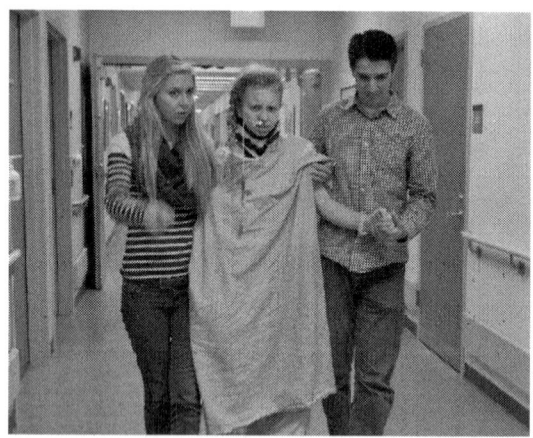

My heart jumped as a wave of joy washed through me. My daughter Cassidy and I cheered loudly, bursting with pride, "Way to go Lexi! Look at you!" Although Lexi was still fairly unstable as she meandered down the hall, it was one of the most poignant moments of my life.

When Lexi got to the end of the hall, her voice cracked with emotion, "I did it." Her face glowed with happiness. By then, my eyes were brimming with tears of joy and my smile stretched wide, basking in the moment. She had never stopped trying, and now she had triumphed! I moved swiftly to her side to embrace her. The warmth of that moment stretched for a long time.

My son JD said it best when describing Lexi's recovery:

"The pain has been almost unbearable at times. She was intubated multiple times, she suffered a broken leg, and the list goes on. Some might ask why God would allow certain people to suffer so much more than others during their life here on earth.

Joseph of Egypt was one who could have asked the same question. Favored by his father, but secretly hated by his brothers, he was sold into Egypt where he became a slave. But instead of dwelling on his misfortune, he went forth until Potiphar made him overseer in his house. He was then cast into prison when Potiphar's wife lied about Joseph's pretended advances toward her. Again instead of turning against the Lord, he turned toward Him. The Lord was with him in prison, and he was able to interpret dreams. At the appropriate time, he was called out to interpret the dream of Pharaoh, and as a result was made second only to Pharaoh in the land. When his brothers came to collect food during the famine, Joseph made himself known to them and said, "Now therefore be not grieved, nor angry with yourselves, that ye sold me hither:

229

for God did send me before you to preserve life" (Genesis 45:5).

At the beginning of Lexi's accident, our family often asked, "Why did this happen to Lexi? She was so good...so young. Why does she have to suffer?" But as time progressed, we realized that God often gives us trials to bless others' lives: "For God did send [Lexi] before [others] to preserve life." Just as Joseph saved thousands during the time of famine, Lexi has given spiritual hope and guidance to our family and friends and, perhaps, has saved a life, spiritually speaking. Our Savior, Jesus Christ, went through the hardest trial ever known to mankind, but through His sacrifice, we all can be saved. What a wonderful thing to know that even trials can be a gift from our Heavenly Father. May our trials turn us to the Lord so that we may bless the lives of others too."

Lexi learned quickly to never ask, "Why did this happen? Why am I in so much pain? Why do I have to learn to walk again?" She trusted in God's plan for her. She never wallowed in self-pity or bitterness but was filled with a quiet determination. When people asked her how she was feeling, there was intensity in her eyes as she would put on her cheery smile and tell them she was doing well. Her words sunk into my thoughts. I knew how agonizing her injuries were, so her answers always surprised me. She didn't want people to worry about her or feel sorry for her. She knew she had been blessed to be alive, and she was grateful for kind friends, brothers and sisters who loved and cared about her.

I love the prophet Nephi because his journey in life was a lot like each of ours is. We all have our bumps and bruises, some more than others, as we are tossed to and fro upon the sea of life. Sometimes we will feel cast aside or forgotten as we "wade through much affliction" (1 Nephi 17:1). Excruciating heat and long, tedious days can be the harsh realities of life, yet despite Nephi's challenges, he says with full faith, "I know in whom I have trusted" (2 Nephi 4:19).

Like Nephi, instead of feeling sorry for herself, Lexi had taken to heart the scripture, "Therefore...let us cheerfully do all things that lie in our power; and then may we stand still with the utmost assurance, to see the salvation of God, and for his arm to be revealed" (D&C 123:17). God would "be with [her] as he was with Moses," and He would "not fail [her] nor forsake [her]" (Joshua 1:17, 5). And as Lexi learned to walk again she continued to walk with God.

CHAPTER TWENTY-THREE

THE MIRACLE OF ARRIVING HOME

"...we must through much tribulation enter into the Kingdom of God." - Acts 14:22

Sitting on the ledge of the eighth-story window was the best vantage point to see the trains. That was important because Calvin, Lexi's two-year-old nephew came to visit her every day, and trains were all he talked about. It didn't hurt that the view from where he perched was spectacular, the snow-capped mountains a stunning backdrop.

My daughter Cassidy, who is Calvin's mom, lived in Texas but had decided to stay for a month in order to help me out and to be there for Lexi. Knowing how hard it must be for a two-year-old to go to the hospital every single day and stay in a cramped, sterile room where he was not allowed to do much of anything, I tried to think of how I could make him happy about returning the following day.

One afternoon I called out to him in an animated voice just as they were leaving the hospital, "Guess what you get to do tomorrow Calvin?"

He glanced over his shoulder to look at me and with eager eyes and said, "What?"

"You get to come to the hospital to see Lexi," I said, trying to put as much expression in my voice as I could.

I was fully expecting him to stomp his feet and tell us he didn't want to come back. But much to my surprise and

relief, he spun around to his mom and squealed with glee, "Yay! We're going to the hospital tomorrow," his sweet expression matching his heart.

To have them come each day created a good diversion for me and helped to break up the monotony. It was also helpful to have someone to voice my concerns to when Lexi was

not moving forward like I wanted. Cassidy, was someone Lexi had always looked up to and thus was also able to give Lex a nod of encouragement when she was about to give up. Lexi had been progressing rapidly physically but she could not swallow without aspirating (inhaling small particles of food or liquid into her lungs), which sentenced her to a longer stint in the hospital.

Each time I thought she conquered her swallowing, she would take a drink, nearly gag, and start to cough over and over again. Her face would fall, a silent sadness in her eyes, and she would sound a sigh of frustration. I tried not to show my disappointment, knowing how

> *"And ye cannot bear all things now; nevertheless, be of good cheer for I will lead you along."* - D&C 78:18

difficult it must be for her to want to leave the hospital and not be able to, but my joy was dashed. She was also anxious to get the feeding tube out and eat real food again, but for the time being she was only allowed ice chips

Two weeks after coming to the rehab center for the third time, she was allowed to eat two spoonfuls of applesauce and two spoonfuls of apple juice two times a day. She was actually given other food options, but she would always ask for the same selection, glance over at me and Cassidy, chuckle, and apologize for doing so. I was pleased at the prospect of her going home soon.

Finally, when I almost did not dare to hope for a departure day, she was able to swallow correctly and the tube was taken out. Relief swept inside me. We both had suppressed the idea that it could happen today, our eyes wide with shock. The best part about passing the swallowing test? She got to come HOME! We were all elated. My heart leaped in my chest, my smile bright.

That same afternoon, she ate her first bite of food. "And this," said Lex scooping up a spoonful of mashed potatoes, "is the greatest day ever."

However, her mouth and head started to pound after eating only a couple bites of food, so she put down her spoon and her gentle smile disappeared. She slouched back down on her pillow, her head throbbing, her body weary. It hurt her to swallow or talk just like even touching her head caused her to wince and cry out. At the moment, I had no idea that getting her to eat would be one of my hardest challenges when she returned home. She was a shadow of her former self.

But we rejoiced that Lexi was going home and knew it was a direct answer to the many prayers given on her behalf.

"..the Spirit of truth, ...will guide you into all truth. ...and he will shew you things to come." - John 16:13.

My friend Elena was one of those people and is a lady of great faith. The night after Lexi's accident she knelt down to pray for Lexi before getting into bed. However in the middle of the night she was awakened and told that Lexi was in need of her prayers again. After praying the second time, she climbed back into bed only to be awakened a short time later with the same prompting--that Lexi's condition necessitated additional prayers. For the third time that night, Elena was obedient to the voice she heard and didn't hesitate to get out of bed to pray for Lexi. When she finished her last prayer, the Spirit told her that Lexi would be made whole and would be home in exactly one month from the accident.

The rays of the sun seeping through the window awakened Elena and her husband in the wee morning hours, and she immediately told him about what she had experienced during the night and the promise given to her. He responded with great skepticism, "Elena I know that you have had many spiritual experiences in the past, but I'm sorry, this time it is not going to happen. Lexi is not supposed to survive, and, even if by some great fortune that she does live, she will not be able to ever walk or talk again. That is what the doctors have told her family."

"No, Steve," she said. "That's what I've been told." She refused to listen to his doubts. True to the revelation Elena was given, in exactly one month's time from the accident Lexi came home from the hospital.

There was a surge of excitement in the rehab center the next day as Lexi got ready to go home. Her favorite song began playing over the loud speaker as her nurse wheeled her around the facility to wave goodbye to nurses, speech, occupational and physical therapists, and staff who had lined the hallway to wish her well and give one last hug.

I was overjoyed to take Lexi home, but it was also heartwarming to see those that had become such a big part of our lives. They had cared for my daughter like their own with cheerful hearts and kindness during monotonous and sometime dreary days. I hoped that I had conveyed my appreciation to them sufficiently. It had been an epic struggle to get her this far, but she made it.

We lingered at the elevator doors allowing Lexi time to etch in her mind the enormity of what was taking place before our descent. As the heavy glass doors slid open, my heart quickened. A rush of fresh air filled our lungs. There was the smell of spring in the air which brought a feeling of hope and a newness of life. The bright sunshine swept over us and through us, reminding us of His son that had brought to us this miracle.

The ride home, however, was anything but kind. Every little bump and jostle of the car caused Lexi to cry out in pain. I drove as slowly as possible, but to Lexi the trip was excruciating. When we pulled up to our house, I had Lexi sit up. She peered out the car window and saw the hundreds of colored ribbons neighbors and friends had tied to our bushes and trees. They had done this a few days after the accident in the pouring rain at a time when they felt she would not ever be coming home. It was a welcoming sight that allowed her to see that she was loved and cared about.

I tenderly and carefully helped her out of the car and into the house where she was greeted by her sister Cassidy and the welcome home posters she had made. We relished the moment. It would have been fun to have friends and neighbors greet her, but her frail body wouldn't have been able to handle it. That day would have to wait.

Although Lexi was steadily getting better, it would not be an easy recovery for her to get back the abilities that she had before. But no matter how slow the progress, Lexi kept trying, kept moving forward. Even though she had to drop out of school and could not walk fast, run or jump, and still had lingering pain, she was holding fast to hope and cherishing every new day she had been given.

The day after Lexi returned home, I became her physical, speech, and occupational therapist. I had taken my oldest daughter Shae to similar therapists on a weekly basis

> *"Beloved, think it not strange concerning the fiery trial which is to try you, as though some strange thing happened unto you: But rejoice, inasmuch as ye are partakers of Christ's sufferings; that, when his glory shall be revealed, ye may be glad also with exceeding joy." - 1 Peter 4:12-13*

and, in addition, had gone with Lexi to all of her sessions, so I felt confident I could do it. I also knew how excruciating it would be for Lexi to travel in a car again, so staying at home was the best option.

Lexi's clothes were still in boxes that had been retrieved from her dorm. I decided this would be a good way to help her to facilitate greater mobility, so I playfully asked her, "Lex, would you put your clothes away as part of your therapy?"

"Nah, I don't mind," Lexi said, shrugging her shoulders. She selected a blue and white flowered blouse, lifting it from the container. But this proved to be quite the formidable task for her.

"I can't do this," Lexi said with teary eyes. She slunk down and collapsed in a heap on the carpet after putting away only three shirts.

I crouched down beside her, drawing my knees beneath my chin, and reached over to rub her arm in sympathy. "Lexi, I've seen you do more than this at the hospital," I said as I tried to prod her on.

But she just sat and moaned, "I'll try tomorrow. Tomorrow I'll be able to." She blew out her breath in frustration and shot me a pleading look.

I hesitated only for a moment. Keeping busy was paramount. "Just put four more items away. You can do hard things," I reminded her. "Don't give up."

Her left eyebrow arched. "Are you sure?" she asked. But my suggestion was enough of an encouragement for her to gingerly sit back up. She reached in the box to retrieve a pair of socks and put them away. It took only a few more minutes before she crumpled on the floor again, her body spent. She grimaced momentarily, as if sudden pain shot through her.

The next morning, I stood in the doorway surveying Lexi's silhouette sleeping soundly in the dim light. I swallowed quickly. I hated to wake her from her slumber, knowing the only relief from the throbbing and intense agony was sleep. She savored the time she had to stay in bed. I gently stroked her forehead knowing how it soothed her agony and quietly whispered her name. Blinking her eyes open and stretching her arms, she winced in pain.

We talked for ten minutes before I asked, "Are you ready to sit up now?"

"No," she shook her head emphatically, hugging her soft pillow tightly. "Just give me a few more minutes," she pleaded, fear mingling with unforgotten pain.

While waiting for her to sit up, it occurred to me that this would be a good time to work on her speech therapy.

"What's the capital of Utah?" I asked, trying to jog her memory.

Lexi looked up and rolled her eyes. "Salt Lake. Duh."

"Sorry, Lex, but you know I have to ask." I knew she didn't like my endless round of questioning, but her memory had not completely returned yet.

"OK, fine," I said, "I will make it more difficult...hmmm... let's see...OK, I've got one: who was the confederate general in the Civil War?"

There was a long questioning look. "I… um… I know the answer. It's just sometimes my mind just won't tell me." Her eyes filled with frustration

"It's OK, we'll come back to it later," I replied, squeezing her arm and continued questioning.

After a half hour of interrogating her, I kindly but firmly insisted she sit up. I refused to let her believe that this was insurmountable.

"But it hurts too much," she cried. Her red, tear-rimmed eyes pleaded up at me. "Let me stay here a little longer pleeasse?" It took a little more coaxing before Lexi took a deep breath and sighed, "OK, I can do this."

Little by little, her pain decreased, although it was hard to see any improvement day to day. Both of us had to put our trust in God.

On Mother's Day, when I walked in her room eating a bowl of cereal, Lexi started to cry. I assumed her tears came because of her head wound, but through her whimpering she managed to tell me that she had wanted to fix me breakfast for Mother's Day. She was distraught and would not be consoled until I suggested that she fix me lunch. Once again, I reflected on the fact that even during her difficult days she was able to look outward to see what she could do to brighten another person's life.

As she improved physically, Lexi was excited to pull her violin out of its case and play again. But her dreams of having a command of the instrument right away were squashed once she started to play. She handed me her violin and crumpled in a heap on the floor.

"I can't play," she moaned. "I don't want to start over. That's why..." her voice faded.

"That's why what?" I asked.

"That's why I didn't want to try." Her eyes peered through her tousled hair that had fallen gently across her face.

"Yes, you can," I would remind her. "As long as you keep trying, God will help you. You've been promised." I winked, handing the violin back to her.

"Mmm, sorry. No, I'm not trying again." Her heart felt ripped away from all she'd known and loved. I knew that tomorrow she would be willing to face the formidable mountain and that soon I would hear those melodic songs throughout the house again. She was not a quitter.

For some reason it was easier for her to accept her choppy and mistake-ridden pieces on the piano. After

> *"I can do all things through Christ which strengtheneth me." - Philippians 4:13*

practicing just a few short weeks, it happened: I was upstairs when a familiar sound warmed my heart. I could faintly hear a beautiful sound flooding into my upstairs bedroom, when it dawned on me that it was Lex playing the piano as serenely as she had before the accident. I flew downstairs carefully so as not to disturb her and edged toward the piano. She was pouring her soul into her music as her slender fingers seemed to dance across the ivory keys. When she was finished, I clapped wildly and wrapped my arms around her squeezing her tight.

"You did it," I said. "It came back. God keeps his promises." A smile broke across her face, realizing what she had accomplished.

The summer flew by despite the long grueling days of therapy. Lexi was excited to return to BYU and show that she could make it on her own. I wasn't worried about her--well maybe I had just a twinge of concern--but I knew I'd miss her fiercely. I had spent the last six months taking care of her, and

 now I had to relinquish my role. These long days together made me even more reluctant for her to leave. But she was ready to face whatever the world was to toss her way.

Once back on campus, the class work proved to be much more difficult than Lexi had anticipated. She began to

wonder as the semester progressed if she would pass some of

her writing classes. But with some extra tutoring and lots of individual effort she made it through.

"...for the Lord seeth not as man seeth: for man looketh on the outward appearance but the lord looketh on the heart." - 1 Sam. 16:7

Now that she was back at BYU, I was simultaneously thrilled but a tad worried about how she'd feel about herself now that her once-flawless face was disfigured. It was remarkable that she didn't receive any cuts or even a tiny scratch on her entire body when she was

hit, yet her whole face was scarred from her chin to her forehead. When the doctors suggested we go to a plastic surgeon in a year, Lexi scoffed at the idea.

"If people don't like me with my scars, then I don't want them for my friends anyway," she said defiantly. I was surprised and delighted by her candid response. She believed it was her spirit and who she had become on the inside that was important.

Before the accident, she seemed oblivious to the fact that she was beautiful. The truth was her striking blue eyes, golden skin, tall thin frame, glistening blond hair that reached half-way down her back, and radiant smile made her drop-dead gorgeous. Yet she was humble and untouched by this gift. She had always had the natural ability to think of others before herself. For teenagers, stylish clothes are an important status symbol, yet Lexi was disinterested in shopping and buying name brand clothes. She wore a pair of shoes that were torn and ripped her entire senior year in high school, but  she didn't care. Looking back at her nonchalant attitude towards her looks, I shouldn't have been surprised by her stance now. She had always felt at home in her own skin.

CHAPTER TWENTY-FOUR

THE MIRACLE OF FOLLOWING HIS FOOTSTEPS

"Jesus commanded his disciples to go "unto the uttermost part of the earth" and bear witness of Him". - Acts 1:8

One day shortly after Lexi's release from the hospital, I walked in the kitchen to see Lexi hunched over and shuffling her feet as she circled around and around our kitchen table.

"What are you doing?" I asked her.

"My friend said that they won't let me go on a mission unless I can walk eleven hours a day. I'm...practicing...I want to go NOW," she said with determination.

I couldn't believe her single-mindedness; she was impatient with her body's limitations and pushed herself to her limits. She continued to limp along for a few more minutes, and then meandered over to the couch and slithered down into its comfort.

"..His word was in [her] heart as a burning fire shut up in [her] bones, and [she] was weary with forbearing, and [she] could not stay." (Jeremiah 20:9)

"I'm not really tired," she announced, trying to hide her fatigue. "My head just hurts." She looked exhausted, a faraway look in her eyes.

She had been begging me for days to take her to the doctor to get a physical so she could leave on her mission, but she knew that I would not take her looking so feeble. I was extremely proud of her drive, yet I still could not

> *"For thus saith the Lord God: Behold, I even I, will both search my sheep, and seek them out." - Ezk. 34:11*

help smiling when I thought of what she might look like to an outside observer. I'm sure they would have called her foolish for even thinking of serving a mission, yet we both knew that she would go and that it would not be long until those promises were fulfilled that were given to her from God's mouthpiece.

Lexi would not relent and insisted I get an appointment to see her doctor that week, even though she had just gotten her neck brace off the week before - just two months after the accident. She still could not move her head without moving her entire body.

At our appointment, the first thing the doctor had her do was lie down on the examination table and try to lift her head up off the table. She couldn't do it. This doctor had never seen

Lexi before and after reading the report about her accident and seeing how frail she was, he told her she could only serve a mission from home and probably not for at least another year.

I told him emphatically that she had been promised in priesthood blessings that she would make a full recovery and serve. Not knowing if he believed in God or not, my voice rang with confidence when I told him about the miracles that had transpired in the last few months.

He got teary eyed and said with reverence, "OK, then we will make it happen." He continued, "You come back in a month, and we will see where you are."

> *"How beautiful upon the mountains are the feet of him that bringeth good tidings, that publisheth peace; that bringeth good tidings of good, that publisheth salvation..." - Isaiah 52:7*

In one month's time, Lexi had improved so rapidly that she was able to drive herself to the doctor's office. The change was dramatic.

"You are a miracle," he said, his voice filled with emotion when he saw her. "You were saved for someone. You have full clearance to go on a mission."

A whisper of a smile crept across Lexi's face. After getting the OK to go from this doctor, she then went to each one of her former doctors and got full clearance to serve with no restrictions.

A week after Lexi had submitted her mission papers[23], she was driving home from work and thought, "Hey, it's Wednesday my call[24] *could* be here, but I'm guessing it won't since they told me it would take 6 weeks longer than everyone else due to my accident. But still...."

> *"Follow me, and I will make you fishers of men."*
> *- Matthew 4:19*

With a little bit of hope, she opened the mailbox, timidly peering inside. The envelope was there! A rush of emotion swept over her and she ran inside screaming, "It came! It came!"

Gladness welled up inside me seeing the light of happiness that sprang from her eyes. It was torturous to wait until the last rays of the sun had slipped behind the mountains signaling the time when family and friends were to arrive to watch her open her call.

Finally the long anticipated hour came, and I was still fighting hard to maintain a calm demeanor. As Lexi stood up in front of the large group, a sudden burst of emotion washed over her and tears filled her eyes as she began to read her letter from the prophet. Her voice

---

[23] Her application to serve a mission for the Church of Jesus Christ of Latter-day Saints

[24] Letter stating where she was assigned to serve

was full of fervor, yet trembling slightly, she told the group assembled that she had been called to serve in Hong Kong, China.

She held back a grin that was threatening to erupt. The

room exploded with cheers and applause. Then, she burst out laughing, "Just kidding! I'm going to Des Moines Iowa."

There was a deafening silence, confused faces staring up at Lexi before realizing they had been duped. Then the room erupted with laughter.

Joy engulfed her as she squealed, "I'm going on a

> *"...when thou are converted strengthen thy brethren." - Luke 22:32*

mission!!!" She didn't care where she was called to serve as long as she was going.

And to make it even more poignant, her lifetime dream of a mission had come on the six month anniversary of her accident. We had not anticipated this joyous day to come so soon. My spirit was soaring. She told me later that it was probably the happiest and most exciting day of her life because she would have a chance to share with others the joy and the comfort she had received through living the gospel.

When Jesus "passed through Jericho...there was a man named Zacchaeus...and he sought to see Jesus...and could not for the press..." (Luke 19:1-3). So too, Lexi found the press of her problems could have kept her from seeing the Savior. But she was like Zacchaes, who did not just stand there in the crowd as it surged. He took matters into his own hands so that he could see the Savior, and "he ran before, and climbed up into a sycamore tree to see him" (Luke 19:4). He knew he was to "act for [himself] and not to be acted upon" (2 Nephi 2:26). It was after he had done his part that the Savior "looked up, and saw him, and said unto him, Zacchaeus, make haste, and come down; for today I must abide at thy house" (Luke 19:5). Obviously the Savior, who knows all things, could have spied Zacchaeus in the crowd, but, just as the women with the issue of blood did, he had to show the Lord through his faith or movement that he would do whatever it took to be near to Him.

Lexi had a press of health problems that could have kept her from going on a mission. She could barely walk, eating made her throat and head hurt, and there was always that excruciating pounding in her head. Notwithstanding all of that, she kept walking, moving and pressing forward, showing to the

251

Lord that she would climb that sycamore tree. When God saw her devotion, he called up to her, looking at her clear blue eyes and said, "Lexi come down and sup with me." Locking her eyes with the Savior she "made haste, and came down, and received him joyfully" (Luke 19:6). No more would I miss an opportunity to sup with the Savior.

CHAPTER TWENTY-FIVE

THE MIRACLE THAT GOD KNOWS US BY NAME

"For I am God, and mine arm is not shortened; and I will show miracles, signs, and wonders, unto all those who believe on my name. And whoso shall ask it in my name in faith, they shall cast out devils; they shall heal the sick; they shall cause the blind to receive their sight, and the deaf to hear, and the dumb to speak, and the lame to walk." - Doctrine and Covenants 35:8-9.

Has it not been remarkable to take this journey with me as we have acknowledged the hand of heaven in Lexi's life?

Some people might say that miracles don't happen in our day. But the God we worship is the same God who healed the lame, gave sight to the blind, and restored hearing to the deaf. Should we not expect that God wants to bless us as much as he did those who lived before us? Paul teaches that we should "seek the Lord, if [we] are willing to find him, for he is not far from every one of us" (Joseph Smith Translation, Acts 17:27).

The parting of the Red Sea provided undeniable evidence of God's divine intervention and the raising of Lazarus reminds us of his power and love. The miraculous healing of Lexi tells us that God's hand is still in our lives that he is aware of us and that all blessings come through him. I could not remain silent when I was literally eye witness to a miracle.

Sometimes when we don't see miracles in our own lives we question, "Heavenly Father are you really there?" We might feel forsaken and lose hope if there is silence in the heavens. But we are not alone. God is refining our souls and

> "...surely the thing God enjoys most about being God is the thrill of being merciful, especially to those who don't expect it and often feel they don't deserve it." - Jeffrey R. Holland, "The Laborers in the Vineyard," Ensign, May 2012

stretching our faith to see if we will remain obedient. So "why should we mourn [or fear] or think our lot is hard? 'Tis not so; all is right. Why should we think to earn a great reward, If we now shun the fight? Gird up your loins; fresh courage take. Our God will never us forsake" ("Come, Come Ye Saints," Hymns, no.30. LDS hymn book. Text: William Clayton, 1814-1879. Music: English folk song). God allows us, at times to struggle on our own so that we can become stronger and better than we were. Eventually, after painful and what may seem like endless tutoring, He will bring light to our difficult days and peace to our troubled souls. We will be OK because God *will* provide a way.

The Lord didn't put any of us on Earth to be free of trials, because it's only through adversity that we can become humble and teachable. Our hearts more readily turn to the Lord knowing that He is the only one that can understand our pain and heartache. He has suffered for us so He can succor us through our personal trials. We cannot do it alone. We must learn to rely on Him and use these trials to change our natures as God "[refines us]…in the furnace of affliction" (Isaiah 48:10).

When adversity comes, we cannot afford to turn away from God. God knows what is needed for our growth in order for us to become like Him. We need to trust in His plan for us, and listen to the spirit even when our prayers aren't answered as we would like or in the time frame we would want. We must learn to live the words, "Trust in the Lord with all thine heart; and lean not unto thine own understanding. In all thy ways acknowledge him, and he shall direct thy paths" (Proverbs 3:5-6).

Do we have confidence that the Lord will deliver us in our darkest nights? Do we believe "He shall feed his flock like

> *"And I will also be your light in the wilderness; and I will prepare the way before you, if it so be that ye shall keep my commandments; wherefore, inasmuch as ye shall keep my commandments ye shall be led towards the promised land; and ye shall know that it is by me that ye are led.*
> *Yea, and the Lord said also that: After ye have arrived in the promised land, ye shall know that I, the Lord, am God; and that I, the Lord, did deliver you from destruction; yea, that I did bring you out of the wilderness."*
> *- 1 Nephi 17:13-14*

a shepherd: he shall gather the lambs with his arm, and carry them in his bosom, and shall gently lead [them]"? (Isaiah 40:11). Will we stand with Shadrach, Meshach, and Abed-nego and say, "I know our God will deliver us, *but if not* I will continue to look upward and trust that He will open a way even when there doesn't appear to be one?"

We are the Lord's sheep, and "he calleth his own sheep by name, and [herein lies our answer] leadeth them out" (John 10:3). He not only hears our prayers, but He will lead us out of our troubles. He will answer us because He has told us "before [we] call [He] will answer; and while [we] are yet speaking, [He] will hear" (Isaiah 65:24). But we need to have the courage to wait for His timetable. Then someday soon, when we kneel at the Savior's feet, we will hear His words, "Well done, thou good and faithful servant" (Matthew 25:21).

The Miracle That God Knows Us by Name

I know that this miracle was not a once-in-a-lifetime event. I believe the Lord sends small miracles to us daily. Look for them each day, and write them down so that you can always remember that God is still a God of miracles.

THE MIRACLE OF ALWAYS
REMEMBERING

"When your children shall ask their fathers in time to come, saying, What mean these stones? Then ye shall let your children know, saying, Israel came over this Jordan on dry land. For the Lord your God dried up the waters of Jordan from before you, until ye were passed over... That all the people of the earth might know the hand of the Lord, that it is mighty." - Joshua 4:21-24

We read in the scriptures how Christ performed miracles daily among the people. And like those who were witnesses, some of you may have had your hearts "burn within [you]" (Luke 24:32) as you've read through these pages. It is the power of the Holy Ghost testifying to you that Lexi's healing was a miracle in our day and that God is still a God of miracles.

Satan doesn't want us to remember. He doesn't want us in a higher place of peace, unspeakable joy, with an unshakable faith in God and His plan for us. We read in the New Testament and in other scriptures of miracles wrought, and yet we find that in just a few short years those same people forgot the miracles and hardened their hearts.

For example, in the Book of Mormon we read that "there began to be lyings sent forth among the people by Satan to harden their hearts to the intent that they might not believe in those signs and wonders which they had seen" (3 Nephi 1:22). And "the people began to forget those signs and wonders which they had heard ... and they began to be hard in their hearts and blind in their minds and began to disbelieve all which they had heard and seen" (3 Nephi 2:1).

So let us "take heed...and keep [our souls] diligently, lest [we] forget the things which [our] eyes have seen and lest they depart from [our hearts]...but teach them to [our] sons, and [our] sons' sons" (Deuteronomy 4:9) and "walk with [Him]" (Moses 6:34) through sunshine and storms.

When Christ asked the apostles who the people thought He was, they answered, "John the Baptist, Elias or one of the prophets." Then the Savior asked Peter, "Whom say ye that I am?" Peter answered, "Thou art the Christ." Yet the night of the Savior's crucifixion, Peter denied the Savior three times. It wasn't until after the Savior was resurrected that Peter's testimonies became unshakable. Through Lexi's miracle I can understand in a very small way the change that came over Peter. I thought I knew God before, but I truly know him now. I have "searched the prophets" and have had "many revelations…and having all these witnesses [I have obtained] a hope, and [my] faith [has become] unshaken" (Jacob 4:6).

Why did this miracle occur? Why are miracles recorded in the scriptures? John tells us why: "But these are written, that ye might believe that Jesus is the Christ, the Son of God; and that believing ye might have life through his name" (John 20:31).

We cannot be the same again. We must not be the same again.

Questions for Personal Reflection and Discussion

1. **What have you learned through God's miraculous preservation of Lexi's life**? Have you felt any specific messages from God personally to you? What is it that He is trying to teach you?

2. **What is the purpose of trials?** How are they a part of God's love and mercy? What is it about trials that helps us grow? What can we do to allow our trials to draw us closer to God instead of push us farther away from Him? What trials in your life have drawn you closer to God?

3. **What is the purpose of a miracle?** Why did this miracle occur in Lexi's life? What are the other miracles that occurred as a result of Lexi's accident? Is a change of heart a greater miracle than that of physical healing?

4. **How has reading this book changed the way you view prayer?** How have you become more assertive in your prayers? Why is there so much power in gratitude

prayers? And why were so many people involved in praying for Lexi?

5. **How can you apply the principles in this book to your life?** What concepts or principles from the book will be most memorable to you? What changes have you made or goals have you set for yourself as a result of what you have read and felt?

61501039R00156

Made in the USA
Lexington, KY
13 March 2017